★ ★ ★ ★ ★ ★ ★ ★ ★ ★ ★ ★ ★ ★ ★ ★ ★ ★ ★ ★

GREAT CIVIL WAR PROJECTS
You Can Build Yourself

Maxine Anderson

nomad press

Nomad Press

A division of Nomad Communications

10 9 8 7 6 5 4 3 2

Copyright © 2005 by Nomad Press

ISBN: 0-9749344-1-0

Questions regarding the ordering of this book should be addressed to

Independent Publishers Group

814 N. Franklin St.

Chicago, IL 60610

www.ipgbook.com

Nomad Press

2456 Christian St.

White River Junction, VT 05001

www.nomadpress.net

Photo credits

Cover: Drums photograph courtesy of Michael K. Sorenson; Grant Library of Congress.

All images other than the ones listed here are courtesy of the Library of Congress:

http://memory.loc.gov/ammem/cwphtml/cwphome.html;

Pg. 15: Johnny Shiloh: www.cs.amedd.army.mil/rlbc/clem.htm; **Pgs. 33–35:** www.history.navy.mil;

Pgs. 46, 47: www.history.navy.mil; **Pg. 47:** Paddlewheeler:

www.usgennet.org/usa/in/county/vanderburgh/postcards/evansville_steamer.jpg;

Pg. 51: www.navymedicine.med.navy.mil; **Pg. 66:** www centennialofflight.gov;

Pg. 83: Flag images courtesy of SCA, www.civilwarsignals.org;

Pg. 88: letters: www.bee.net; **Pg. 106:** www.civilwartheater.com; **Pgs. 114–116:** Fashion illustrations courtesy Son of the South www.sonofthesouth.net; **Pg. 119:** banjo player: home.versateladsl.be

CONTENTS

ACKNOWLEDGMENTS

This book would not have been possible without the help, wisdom, and experience of many people. I would like to thank Duncan Trussell from the National Civil War Museum for his comments and ideas, especially for the battlefield sections; Dr. James McPherson of Princeton University for his precise review of the manuscript and corrections and suggestions for improvement in several areas; Dr. James Weeks at *Civil War Times* for his kind words of encouragement; Don Wickman of the Woodstock, Vermont Historical Society for his comments and review; Michael K. Sorenson for his generosity in allowing Nomad Press to use images from his private collection of Civil War memorabilia; and Corin Hirsch, who designed a terrific cover. Special thanks to everyone at Nomad Press for their hard work and commitment to making *Great Civil War Projects You Can Build Yourself* the best book it could be: Sarah, Jeff, Susan, David, Rachel, Alex, Mark, Eric, and Lauri. And finally, to Byron Phillip Anderson—thanks for everything, as always.

INTRODUCTION

Have you ever wondered what life would be like if you had lived during the Civil War? A lot would depend on who you were and where you lived: if you were white or black, a farmer or a city dweller, or if you were rich or poor before the Civil War started. But whether you lived in the Deep South or Far North, whether your hometown was the site of a battle or far removed from any fighting at all, there is no question you would have been greatly affected by the conflict between the Union and Confederate armies.

This book will help you discover a bit about what life was like during the Civil War for families, soldiers, and children. You'll learn a little history of why the Civil War began, some interesting facts about the people, places, and battles during the war, and create projects that will give you an idea of what people during the Civil War did to communicate, have fun, and live their day-to-day lives. The book is divided into three general sections: **On The Battlefield** covers projects that deal with a soldier's life in camp and during battle. **On The Homefront** features projects that give you an idea of what life was like for everyday people during the Civil War.

Most of the projects in this book can be made by kids with minimal adult supervision, and the supplies needed are either common household items or easily available at craft stores. So, take a step back into the 1860s and get ready to **Build It Yourself**.

HOW IT ALL BEGAN

The Civil War, or the War Between the States, as it is sometimes called, officially began on April 12, 1861, at a place called Fort Sumter in South Carolina. The Confederate army attacked the fort, which belonged to the Union, for two solid days, until finally the Union soldiers surrendered the fort to the Confederacy. This was the first

battle of a war that would last for four years and cost more than a half million lives, but the reason for the war started much earlier— some would say as far back as the founding of the United States almost 100 years before those first shots were fired.

So what was the cause of the war? In a word, slavery. When the founders of the United States got together back in 1787 to write the U.S. Constitution, the document that sets up the rules for how our country is governed, they decided that in order to get everyone to agree on a basic set of laws to rule the country they would need to include

CONFEDERATE: *The government established by the southern states of the United States, called the Confederate States of America, after they seceded from the Union in 1860 and 1861.*

UNION: *The United States, especially the northern states during the American Civil War.*

FEDERAL: *Having to do with the northern United States and those loyal to the Union during the Civil War; also a member of the Union army.*

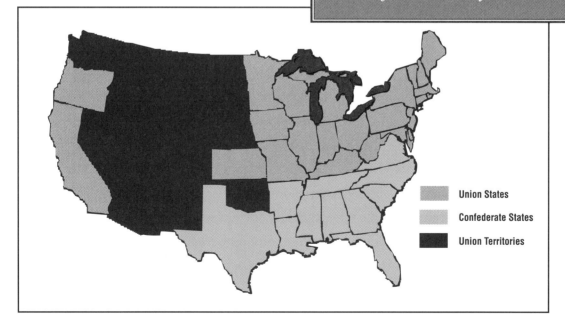

Union States
Confederate States
Union Territories

Slave auction.

some rules about slavery. Since slavery was already an important part of the South's way of life and vital to its economy, the founders of the country realized they would need to allow slavery in certain parts of the country so that the leaders of the South would agree to the Constitution as the law of the land.

So in the end, the Constitution declared that in states where slavery was legal when the Constitution was written, slavery would remain legal. They also agreed that the slave trade could continue until 1808, and that a slave could not become free by escaping to another state. But the Constitution also stated that each time a new state wanted to join the Union, the people voting to become a state would have to decide for themselves whether or not to allow slavery in that new state.

Over the next eighty or so years, every time a new state entered the Union, the debate about slavery came up again and again. Existing states worried that the balance of power between free states and slave states would become uneven—if too many free states joined the Union, the slave states thought, then they would have enough power to make slavery illegal everywhere. If too many slave states joined the Union, thought the free states, the slave states would have enough power to make slavery legal everywhere.

Over the years some unfortunate compromises were made so that the balance of free states and slave states stayed equal: the Missouri Compromise in 1820 brought Missouri into the Union as a slave state, and Maine into the Union as a free state. The Missouri Compromise also made it illegal to have slaves in all federal territories that were part of the Louisiana Purchase north of the latitude that formed Missouri's southern border. The Compromise of 1850 brought California into the Union as a free state, but also passed a new and stronger Fugitive Slave Act—which meant that by law, any runaway slaves found in any part of the country, whether they were free states or slave states, had to be returned to their owners. The situation was balanced, but tense.

Finally, an 1857 decision by the United States Supreme Court called the Dred Scott decision brought a whole new level of conflict to the slavery issue. The Dred Scott decision ruled that no one, not Congress or any territorial government, could outlaw or prohibit slavery in any federal territory. That meant that anyone who was a slave owner could bring his slaves with him to any of the land in the United States that wasn't already officially a state (which is why they were called territories) and still legally own them, even if the territory was considered a "free territory."

This is when things got violent: the Southern states wanted to expand slavery into the new territories that were opening up in the West, and the Northern states wanted to prohibit slavery to keep the balance equal between slave and free states. Now remember that in 1857 the United States was the same physical size as it is today, but had only 31 states: most of the land in the middle and western half of the country was divided into territories, rather than official states, so there was a lot of open space to work with. The territories out west were very appealing to big Southern planters: their own soil had been over-planted and was no longer productive, and they wanted new territories to remain open to slavery so they could move the cotton industry to new, fertile soil.

The slave vs. free state issue came to a violent head when the Kansas territory had the opportunity to vote itself into the Union as either a free state or a slave state. People from outside the state on both sides of the issue raced to Kansas to try to influence the vote, and people on both sides ended up in violent clashes. Kansas territory became known as "Bleeding Kansas" because of so many bloody battles between people who supported Kansas as a slave state, and people who supported Kansas as a free state. The Kansas issue took so long to resolve, in fact, that it didn't become a state until 1861, when the rest of the country was splitting apart at the seams over slavery. Kansas eventually voted to become a free state, but by then the entire country was at the brink of war with itself.

By the time the presidential election of 1860 came around, the Southern states were ready to split from the Union. They said that they didn't want to be part of a Union where one central government made all the rules for the entire country; rather, each state in the South wanted to be able to make their own laws and enforce them as they saw fit, which meant that if that state wanted to make slavery legal, it could. Southern states were sure that the Federal candidate, Abraham Lincoln, was anti-slavery and would restrict the future expansion of slavery as the first stop toward its "ultimate extinction," as Lincoln once put it, if he was elected.

When Lincoln won the election in November 1860, the Southern states decided that they had had enough of being part of the Union. A month after Lincoln's election, South Carolina seceded from the United States, followed shortly after by Florida, Mississippi, Alabama, Louisiana, Georgia, and Texas. These states formed their own country, the Confederate States of America. They were eventually joined by Virginia (the eastern half), Tennessee, Missouri, and Kentucky. The Confederate states elected Jefferson Davis as its president on February 4, 1861, and two months later, the first shots of the Civil War were fired.

Jefferson Davis (l)
Abraham Lincoln (r)

CIVIL WAR TIMELINE

November 1860 Abraham Lincoln is elected President of the United States. Lincoln is against the spread of slavery to new territories in America, and many Southern states think he is a threat to their way of life.

December 1860 South Carolina secedes from the Union.

Early 1861 Six more Southern states—Mississippi, Alabama, Florida, Georgia, Texas, and Louisiana—secede from the United States of America and form a new country with its own government and constitution called the Confederate States of America. Jefferson Davis is named its president.

April 1861 Confederate forces capture Fort Sumter in South Carolina from the Union, which starts the Civil War and leads Virginia, North Carolina, Arkansas, and Tennessee to secede from the Union and join the Confederacy. Richmond, Virginia is named the new capitol.

July 1861 In the first major conflict in the Civil War, called the First Battle of Bull Run or the First Battle of Manassas, the Union army is forced to retreat northward toward Washington.

Fall 1861 The Union navy blockades the coastline of the Confederate states to limit their supplies.

May 1862 Confederate General Stonewall Jackson and his troops battle Union forces in the Shenandoah Valley, Virginia, forcing the Union soldiers to retreat across the Potomac to Washington, D.C.

August 1862 The Second Battle of Bull Run or the Second Battle of Manassas is a victory for the Confederacy.

September 1862 Harper's Ferry falls to Confederate troops under the command of General Jackson, leading to the Battle of Antietam, known as the bloodiest day of the war. The battle is not decisive.

January 1863 President Lincoln issues the Emancipation Proclamation, freeing all slaves in the Confederacy.

May 1863 Confederate General Robert E. Lee hands the Union a major loss at the Battle of Chancellorsville, Virginia, but the victory is marred when Stonewall Jackson dies from his wounds a few days later.

July 1863 The Gettysburg Campaign is the turning point of the war, with huge Confederate losses. At the same time Confederates surrender Vicksburg, Mississippi, to General Ulysses S. Grant of the Union army, placing much of the Mississippi River under the control of the Union army and splitting the Confederacy in half.

September 1863 Confederates win the Battle of Chickamauga, Georgia.

November 1863 In the three-day Battle of Chattanooga, Union soldiers take control of the city and ultimately almost all of Tennessee. Lincoln delivers his famous Gettysburg Address at a ceremony dedicating a soldiers' cemetery at the site of the Battle of Gettysburg. It began with the lines, "Four score and seven years ago our fathers brought forth, upon this continent, a new nation, conceived in liberty, and dedicated to the proposition that all men are created equal."

May–June 1864 General Grant leads the Wilderness Campaign, a long and bloody battle. He pursues General Lee's soldiers relentlessly toward Richmond, despite enormous casualties. Grant withdraws toward Petersburg.

August–November 1864 Union General William T. Sherman marches from Chattanooga, Tennessee, to Atlanta, Georgia, taking the city and continuing on to the sea. Abraham Lincoln is re-elected to another term.

January 1865 The United States Congress approves the Thirteenth Amendment to the United States Constitution, abolishing slavery.

April 1865 The Confederate capitol of Richmond, Virginia, falls to Union forces. General Lee surrenders. Less than one week later President Lincoln is shot by John Wilkes Booth.

May 1865 All remaining Confederate troops surrender and Jefferson Davis, president of the Confederate States of America is captured in Georgia.

★ IMPORTANT PEOPLE
Union

Abraham Lincoln: President of the United States from 1861 to 1865. Lincoln won the election of 1860 with fewer than 40 percent of the popular vote, and his election spurred the secession of the Southern states. Lincoln's Emancipation Proclamation in 1863 freed slaves in territories held by the Confederacy, and he is famous today as the president who ended slavery in the United States. He was assassinated by John Wilkes Booth on April 14, 1865.

Ulysses S. Grant: Commander of the Union forces in 1864. Grant was an army officer who left the service in 1854, then rejoined at the start of the Civil War. No one expected very much of him, but he led his troops to several stunning victories on the western front. After taking command of the Union forces Grant was able to defeat the Confederates in less than a year.

Confederacy

Jefferson Davis: President of the Confederate States from 1861 to 1865. Davis had been a U.S. Senator for many years, and was President Franklin Pierce's Secretary of War from 1853 to 1857. He joined the Confederacy hoping for a military command, and was instead elected president by the Confederate Congress. After the Confederacy lost the war Davis spent two years in prison, after which the charges of treason against him were dropped. He died in 1899.

Robert E. Lee: Commander of the Army of Northern Virginia, the pre-eminent Confederate Army. Lee was asked by President Lincoln in 1861 to command the Union Army. He declined, and instead took command of the Confederate forces. Robert E. Lee was universally liked and respected by both Confederate and Union leaders.

ON THE BATTLEFIELD

Most soldiers who joined up to fight for either the Union or Confederacy had no idea what they were getting themselves into. No one realized that the secession of the Southern states and the first cannon fired at Fort Sumter was heralding the start of a war that would last for four long years, cost more than half a million lives, and ravage much of the southern half of the country.

Neither side was prepared to fight a war: the Union had a small standing army that was immediately cut by large numbers of high-ranking officers who left to join the Confederate army, and while the Union had more weapons than the Confederacy, many of them dated back to the Revolutionary War.

ABOLITIONIST: *someone who believed that slavery should be abolished*

Why did soldiers join either army? In the case of the Confederacy, most wanted to defend their state, their home, and their families. It was clear from the beginning that most of the fighting would take place in the southern half of the country, where the states that had seceded were located. Union soldiers joined up for a variety of reasons: some because they believed in the idea of a single country and national government, some because they believed in the abolitionist cause, and others because they wanted some adventure.

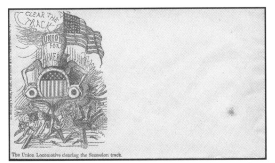

"Clear the Track—Union For Ever," pictorial envelope.

What soldiers on both sides found was nothing that they had experienced before. Most soldiers spent far more time waiting around camp or marching long distances than they did fighting on the battlefield, but when they did fight it was slaughter on a massive scale. In one infamous battle, the Battle of Gettysburg, more than 51,000 men were killed or wounded in the span of only three days. One in four soldiers died during the war, but surprisingly, disease was a far bigger killer than bullet wounds. For every soldier killed in battle, two died of diseases such as dysentery, diarrhea, typhoid, and malaria, mostly due to the crowded and unsanitary living conditions. Soldiers who came from small, rural areas contracted childhood diseases such as measles and chickenpox because they'd never had them before and didn't have immunities to them; more than 5,000 Union soldiers died of measles during the war.

Battlefield medicine was pretty grim: Surgeon General William Hammond called medicine during the 1860s "the end of the Middle Ages." No one had any knowledge about sterilizing instruments or operating areas. In addition, the type of ammunition most commonly used by both armies, called the "minie" ball, was large and made of soft lead, so it distorted on impact, shattering any bones it came in contact with and infecting the wound with clothing, dirt, and debris. The most common method of treating leg or arm wounds was to amputate as soon as possible. It was no wonder that more than 200,000 men died of their battle wounds, usually from shock and infection.

All these injuries led both the Union and Confederate armies to completely change the way they waged war. Old methods of fighting were made obsolete by new kinds of weapons that shot much farther and more accurately than ever before. By the end of the war, four years after it began, siege fighting had taken the place of the old methods that had been in use since the Revolutionary War.

Zouave ambulance crew demonstrating removal of wounded soldiers from the field.
Unknown location.

Soldiers pass the time playing dominoes at a mess table.

Camp life for soldiers was boring and predictable. Much of the soldiers' time was spent drilling (marching in formation) mounting up (preparing to move into battle), and working around camp. For Union soldiers, food and other supplies were usually easily available, and what they weren't assigned they could usually buy at the sutler's wagons just outside of camp. If you were a Confederate, though, you had a much harder go of it: the Confederate army had far fewer supplies, and soldiers often depended on the generosity of family members at home or farmers and businesses near where they were camped.

Soldiers in the Civil War rarely got to go home; most signed up for a first three-month muster, and then when it became clear that the war wasn't going to end in three months, they re-upped for periods of up to three years. About a year into the war the Confederates created a draft, and a year later, the Union did, too.

When the war finally ended in 1865, more than 1.1 million men and boys had been killed or wounded, the South was in ruins, and most soldiers just wanted to go home. Many, though, couldn't forget what they had been through during those five long years, and several years after the war ended soldiers on both sides formed veterans' organizations. For many years, the Grand Army of the Republic (Northern soldiers) and United Confederate Veterans (Southern soldiers) met for reunions. In 1913 more than 54,000 veterans of both organizations met for the largest Civil War veteran's reunion, which coincided with the 50th anniversary of the Battle of Gettysburg.

SIEGE FIGHTING

In earlier wars, battles were fought at close hand and victories and defeats were quick and decisive. New weapons developed during the Civil War changed the methods of battle to what is called siege fighting, where battles lasted for long periods of time—sometimes as long as several months. Troops often dug trenches and fortifications in the ground and stayed in them, fighting only sporadically and waiting for the other side to quit.

BANDS AND MUSIC

Civil War band.

Music played a large role in the lives of Civil War soldiers, both on and off the battlefield. Recruitment rallies always had a military band playing, which inspired many young men to join up, and most volunteer regiments joined up with a complete band of their own. The bands helped boost soldier morale during long marches, serenaded them in camp, and inspired them before, and sometimes during, battles.

The most common kinds of instruments played in regimental and brigade bands during the war were drums and brass instruments, usually bugles, and sometimes fifes. Cavalry and artillery units only used bugles, and the bugler was considered their regimental musician, responsible not only for music, but also for signaling on the battlefield. Individual regiments got so used to hearing their particular bugler play, in fact, that they could tell his bugle calls from any other regiments' bugle calls.

Drummers were vital for battlefield communication. The type of weapons used in the war created huge amounts of smoke, so visibility quickly became very limited. Drummers helped soldiers locate their unit and helped keep the units together. Drums were often the most effective way to relay signals to troops on the battlefield, since during a battle the noise of guns and fighting often drowned out the sound of voices. When soldiers heard a long roll being played by the drummers, they knew that this was a signal to march into combat. Off the battlefield or at camp, three single drumbeats signaled the end of a soldier's day.

KNOW YOUR SLANG

here's your mule—a term the infantry used to insult the cavalry

web feet—a term the cavalry had for the infantry

Later in the war, as the armies changed tactics to a guerilla-type method including trench warfare and smaller, quicker units, they used buglers more and drummers a bit less. In addition to new methods of fighting, the weapons on the battlefield had become more powerful and much louder than at any other time in history, and amid the noise, the drums were hard to hear.

BATTLE OF THE BANDS

Often at sunset, regimental bands on both sides would play songs back and forth to each other, matching each other's playing of a particular song. They often started out with marching music and popular songs, and as the evening wore on, they would play softer, slower songs. It has been documented that in December 1862, a couple of weeks after the Battle of Fredericksburg, which up to that time had been one of the bloodiest battles of the war, 100,000 Union troops and 70,000 Confederate troops were camped on opposite sides of the bank of the Rappahannock River. The regimental bands were playing their usual evening rounds of songs, and as the evening wore on, one of the Union bands started playing "Home, Sweet Home." One by one all the other regimental bands joined in, all other activity in the camps stopped, and all 170,000 men were silent as they listened to the bands play the song. When the song finally ended, there was a moment of silence, and then suddenly both sides started cheering. One soldier wrote, "Had there not been a river between them, the two armies would have met face to face, shaken hands, and ended the war on that spot."

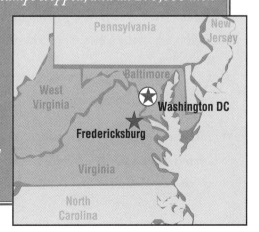

Drum Corps of Sixty-First New York Infantry.

Most of the drummers and buglers in the Civil War were boys, sometimes as young as 11 years old. While each side banned boys from fighting—the Union said recruits had to be 18 and the Confederates also had age limits—the easiest way to sneak into the army was as a drummer or bugler. They were officially "nonfighting" positions so most recruiters let them sign on without too many questions about their age. Since

Bugler.

CIVIL WAR FACTS & TRIVIA

★ *One Union drummer named Orion Howe, who was 14 years old, won the Medal of Honor (which was first given out in the Civil War) for relaying orders on the battlefield even though he was terribly wounded.*

★ *The Union army had more than 40,000 drummers and buglers. The Confederates had 20,000 who served.*

★ *The second role of the musicians during the war was as stretcher bearers. When battles were over the band members were assigned the job of carrying the wounded off the battlefield.*

John Lincoln Clem, nicknamed Johnny Shiloh, age 12, 1863.

most people didn't even have birth certificates, let alone other forms of identification, sneaking into the army on either side wasn't very difficult.

One of the most famous boy soldiers in the Civil War was a drummer named Johnny Clem. He first tried to join the Union army when he was nine, but was turned down, so he ran away from home and attached himself to the Twenty-Second Michigan Infantry Unit. The soldiers in the unit liked him, so they let him stay, chipped in to pay his wages, and even made him a uniform and a cut-down shotgun. He did errands around camp for the soldiers, and they taught him how to be a drummer boy. During the Battle of Shiloh, a shell ripped through his drum, and Johnny Clem was given the nickname Johnny Shiloh. In 1863 the army finally formally allowed him to enlist, and he rose to the rank of general before his career was over. When he died in 1937 he was buried in Arlington National Cemetery.

KNOW YOUR SLANG
fit as a fiddle—in good shape, healthy, feeling good

Drum Corps.

MAKE YOUR OWN CIVIL WAR BUGLE

WHAT YOU'LL NEED

★ **garden hose** (You'll be cutting up the hose, so make sure it's okay with your parents before you start. You can also buy a cheap hose at any discount store for this project.)

★ **kitchen funnel**

★ **duct tape**

★ **garden shears or a sharp knife**

WHAT TO DO

1. Cut about two feet of the nozzle end of the garden hose, keeping the nozzle part on. The nozzle will be your mouthpiece.

2. Coil the hose into one loop with the mouthpiece at one end and the cut end at the other. Duct tape the coil together.

3. Put the funnel on the cut end of the hose. If it is too wide to fit inside the hose, you can duct tape it to the end of the hose.

To play:

In order to play your garden hose bugle (or any brass instrument), you'll need to press your lips together and make a buzzing noise against the mouthpiece. This takes a little practice, but by changing the shape of your mouth while buzzing you can make a lot of different notes. You can even play "Taps" (okay, you won't sound as good as a regular bugle, but the notes will work).

Music for Taps:
GGC GCE GCE GCE GCE
CEG ECG GGC

MAKE YOUR OWN CIVIL WAR DRUM

WHAT YOU'LL NEED

★ **cylindrical container** like a coffee can, oatmeal box, or nut container—different size containers will make different pitches

★ **a piece of paper** large enough to wrap around your container

★ **coloring/decorating materials**

★ **tape or glue**

★ **scissors**

★ **canvas or rubber material or leather** large enough to cover the top and bottom of your container

★ **2 large rubber bands**

★ **wooden spoons, sticks, wooden rods, pencils, or pens** for drumsticks

WHAT TO DO

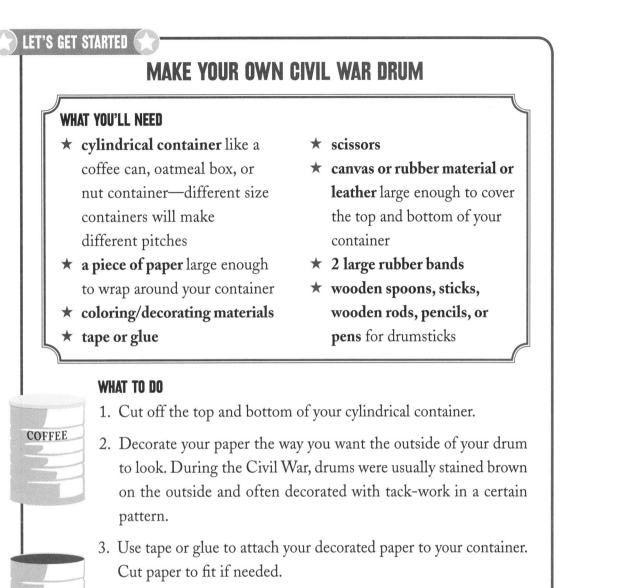

1. Cut off the top and bottom of your cylindrical container.

2. Decorate your paper the way you want the outside of your drum to look. During the Civil War, drums were usually stained brown on the outside and often decorated with tack-work in a certain pattern.

3. Use tape or glue to attach your decorated paper to your container. Cut paper to fit if needed.

4. Take your chosen material for the top and bottom and cut out circular pieces that are larger than the diameter of the container. The pieces should be large enough that an inch or two of material hangs over the edge of the container. During the Civil War, this mate-

Actual Civil War drums.

rial would be made out of calfskin, which stretches easily and is very sensitive to moisture. This was the easiest material to use, as there weren't the man-made materials that we have today.

5. Use the rubber bands to hold the material around the circumference of the container. Pull the material taut so the drum will beat well.

6. You can glue pieces of string or draw dark lines from the top to the bottom in zigzag fashion, creating triangles or parallel lines on the outside of the drum. Civil War drums had these, and they were made with brown or black rope.

7. Now that your drum is complete, play it using your drumsticks.

A possible way to decorate your drum.

PHOTOGRAPHY

ON THE BATTLEFIELD

The Civil War was the first time in American history that photography was extensively used to make a public record of the events that took place. The art of photography was only 21 years old when the Civil War started, but it was already hugely popular in the United States. For the first time, middle class Americans were able to have their portraits taken, since photographs were much less expensive than paintings. Before they left for the war, many Civil War soldiers had their portraits taken by traveling photographers or small photography studios, usually using a type of photography known as ambrotype. Ambrotypes were one-of-a-kind images made on glass or metal and stored in small glass-covered cases.

KNOW YOUR SLANG

somebody's darling—a dead soldier; the name of a popular Civil War song

Photographers not only took portraits of soldiers, they also traveled to camps and battlegrounds, recording the events of the war before and after they took place. Most of these photographs used a wet-plate negative: a glass plate chemically treated, then exposed to the image from 5 to 30 seconds, creating a negative that could be printed on multiple pieces of paper.

Before the camera was used to record the war, images had to be sketched by artists. This one of the battlefield was rendered by John Francis Edward Hillen, 1819–1865.

MATHEW BRADY

The most famous photographer of the Civil War was Mathew Brady, a very successful portrait photographer in New York before the war. Brady photographed many important political leaders and foreign dignitaries in his studio and was one of the first to use photographs as a way to record historical events.

When the Civil War broke out, Brady recruited a group of photographers to travel throughout the United States, making a photographic record of the battles, soldiers, and cities affected by the war. Brady didn't take many of the photographs himself, but every photograph taken by his assistants was credited, "Photo by Brady," making him very famous during the war. He also bought many negatives of war images taken by independent photographers. More than 5,000 images were taken during the Civil War, many of them credited to Mathew Brady.

By the time the war ended, though, Brady had spent almost all of his money and was nearly bankrupt. Worse, as soon as the war was over, so was the interest in his war photographs. Nobody wanted to buy photographs that reminded them of what they had been through so recently, and Brady's negatives were forgotten. Finally, in 1875, Congress paid him $27,840 for the rights to all of his images. Brady died poor and forgotten in 1895, but was buried in Arlington National Cemetery to honor him for his important photographic work during the war.

Mathew Brady

Civil War photographers were not out on the battlefield as fighting was happening; the photographic equipment was bulky and delicate, and the process of exposing and developing the images made it virtually impossible to take action shots. What photographers did instead was to photograph the battlefield after fighting had ended, often before wounded or dead soldiers could be removed to field hospitals. Field photographers were known to rearrange dead bodies on the battlefield to make their shots look more dramatic.

Civil War–era photographer's wagon.

CIVIL WAR FACTS & TRIVIA

★ *Timothy O'Sullivan, one of Mathew Brady's field photographers, took images of the Battle of Gettysburg that were so moving, they inspired Abraham Lincoln's Gettysburg Address.*

★ *Civil War photographer reenactors have resurrected the art of wet-plate photography, making photographs of reenactments in the same way Civil War photographers made their originals.*

★ *Of the thousands of photographs taken during the Civil War, none is of an actual battle in progress.*

MAKE YOUR OWN PINHOLE CAMERA

WHAT YOU'LL NEED

- ★ **film**—one cartridge of 110 size color film, such as Kodak Gold 200
- ★ **ruler**
- ★ **thick corrugated cardboard**
- ★ **scissors**
- ★ **knife**
- ★ **black tape**
- ★ **black paper or black paint**
- ★ **aluminum foil**
- ★ **pencil**
- ★ **pin** (must be straight) or sewing needle
- ★ **two large rubber bands**
- ★ **dime or nickel**

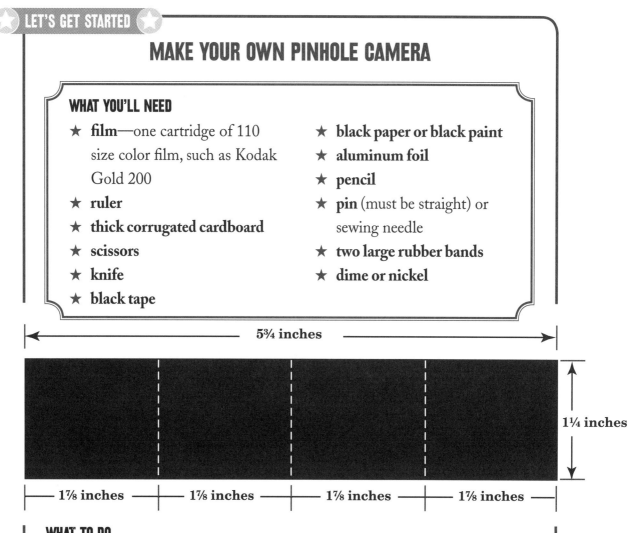

5¾ inches

1¼ inches

1⅞ inches — 1⅞ inches — 1⅞ inches — 1⅞ inches

WHAT TO DO

1. Measure the cardboard to 5¾ inches in length and 1¼ inches in width. Then measure four equal sections of 1⅞ inches in width (see diagram). Use a knife to cut the cardboard slightly (not all the way through) so that it's easier to fold. Fold the cardboard into a box, and tape it with black tape. The inside must also be black, so using the black paper, make a lining for the inside of your box. You can also paint it black.

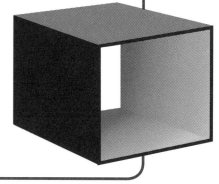

2. Insert the box into the film cartridge, with one of the open sides of the box toward the film cartridge (so that the film cartridge creates a fifth side of the cube). This should be a snug fit.

3. To create the front of the camera, cut another rectangle of cardboard, 2¾ inches by 1½ inches. Line this piece with black paper or paint as well. Cut a square hole ½ inch by ½ inch in the center of this piece of cardboard and tape a 1-inch square of aluminum foil over the hole. Punch a small hole in the foil with the pin, being careful to make it as small as possible.

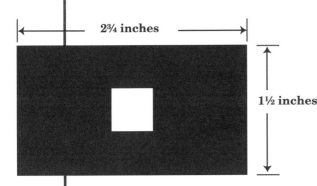

2¾ inches

1½ inches

4. Fasten the front of the camera to the rest of the camera with two strong rubber bands (see diagram).

5. Make sure that no light is leaking into your camera. Use the black tape to cover any holes.

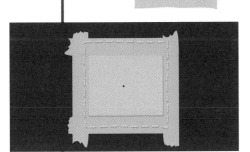

6. When you aren't taking a picture, the hole must be covered by a piece of black paper. This can be done by taping paper over the hole or creating some kind of shutter that slides across the hole.

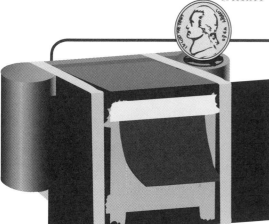

7. Use the dime or nickel to advance the film, turning in a counterclockwise direction. There is a small window on the side of the film cartridge that will indicate the advancing of the film. The film will be in proper position when the numbers 3 and 4 show up in the window.

How to take a picture

- Make sure that the camera is very stable; the best pictures will be produced when the camera doesn't move when the film is being exposed. You can set it on a solid surface such as a chair, table, windowsill, or rock.

- Experiment with different exposure times. One to three seconds should work, but, depending on the amount of sun or light that is available, this time may change. (The film may actually have a recommended exposure time on it.)

- Don't forget to cover the pinhole with black paper after each exposure.

- If you want to ensure that you get a decent image, you may want to take your picture two or three times with different exposure times. The technique of taking three exposures—one with the recommended exposure time, one with twice the time, and one with half the time—is called bracketing.

FLAGS OF THE CIVIL WAR

Flags—often called "colors"—played a very important role during the Civil War for many reasons. They were the symbols of Union sympathizers versus Confederate sympathizers and they demarcated different regiments and groups. They flew above forts, letting people know what group the fort belonged to, and they were carried during battle in order to keep an army together and to serve as a direction marker—where the colors went, the soldiers went, too.

Regimental flags, which were flags representing different groups of soldiers, were vital to keeping the group together on the battlefield, and they also helped to identify the regiment. Confederate regiments usually carried a flag with a specific design that corresponded to the army they were in: if a regiment was in the Army of Northern Virginia, for example, its flag was usually a red square with a Confederate cross (also known as a St. Andrew's Cross) of blue stripes and white stars. Individual regiments would put their regiment number and the initials of their home state on their flag. Some regiments also

Washington, D.C. Signal Corps officers lowering flag at their camp near Georgetown. General Albert J. Myer, in civilian dress, is at right of pole.

THE COLOR GUARD

One of the most important and prestigious jobs a soldier could have was to be part of a regiment's Color Guard—the group of men who carried the colors into battle. Men chosen for the Color Guard were appointed because of bravery or service to their unit. To be chosen for this honor was the equivalent of receiving a medal.

Members of the Color Guard were excused from regular camp duty, but they were expected to lead their regiment into every battle. Their only job was to protect the flag bearer, known as the color sergeant, who was constantly in grave danger; it is said that this was the most dangerous job during the Civil War. If the color sergeant fell and the enemy captured the flag, this was a great triumph for the flag capturers and a terrible loss for the regiment.

put the names of the battles they had fought in on the flag. Union regimental flags and Confederate regimental flags from the deep south and western armies were often very elaborate, ranging from pictures of palmettos, the small palm trees of South Carolina, to the bear of the California 100. It is said that the more regimental colors an army was flying, the greater its strength.

In addition to regimental flags, there were artillery, cavalry, engineer, and hospital flags. Flags were also used as post offices: if a commander needed to get a message to another officer on the battlefield, he knew he could send a rider to the regiment's flag and find the officer nearby.

The following pages will give you the history of and instructions for how to make different Civil War flags, which ranged from very ornate to quite simple. Flags also often went through many changes, as regiments revised their flags in order to unify their group and differentiate their flag from those of other regiments.

THE UNION'S FORT SUMTER FLAG

One of the most famous battles (if not *the* most famous) of the Civil War occurred

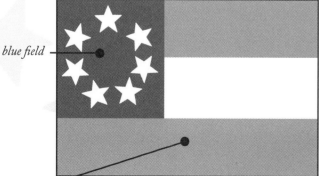

blue field

2 red stripes

"Stars and Bars," the first Confederate flag, adopted March 1861.

blue field

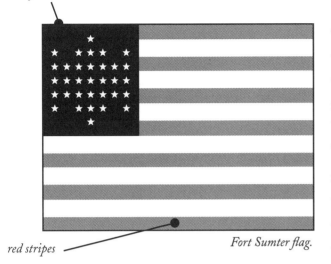

red stripes

Fort Sumter flag.

when Confederate forces in Charleston, South Carolina, attacked Fort Sumter, which was under the control of Union forces. This flag flew at Fort Sumter when Union troops resided there early in 1861. There were 33 stars on this Union flag, representing the 33 states in the Union at that time (as compared to the 50 states today). It was the fifteenth official flag of the United States.

On April 11, 1861, Major Robert Anderson, the man in charge of the Union troops was told to evacuate the fort by General Beauregard of the Confederate army. Anderson refused to evacuate, resulting in a Confederate attack on Fort Sumter headed by Beauregard.

The Confederate troops launched their attack in the early morning hours of April 12. By April 13, the flagstaff and the Union flag had been fired upon and shot down, and the fort was in flames. The Confederates, seeing the flag lowered, believed this signified surrender. As they were rowing a boat over to the fort to evacuate the Union troops, Anderson raised another flagstaff and flag, indicating to the Confederates that this battle was not yet over. It took two more

Fort Sumter with Confederate colors flying.

attacks by the Confederates to weaken Anderson and his troops enough to force their surrender. On April 14, the Union flag was lowered and the Confederate palmetto flag was raised. The Union flag would not be raised above Fort Sumter again until April 14, 1865.

PALMETTO FLAG OF SOUTH CAROLINA

With his surrender at the end of the battle at Fort Sumter, Major Anderson was forced to take the 33-star Union flag down, and the Eighteenth Regiment of South Carolina raised the palmetto flag over Fort Sumter on April 14, 1861. This battle signified the official beginning of the Civil War.

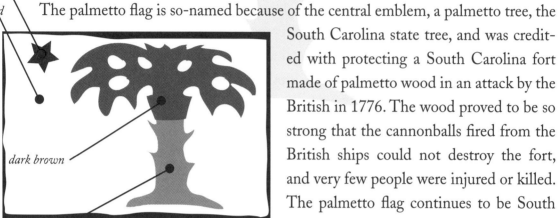

red star

white field

dark brown

light brown

Palmetto flag.

The palmetto flag is so-named because of the central emblem, a palmetto tree, the South Carolina state tree, and was credited with protecting a South Carolina fort made of palmetto wood in an attack by the British in 1776. The wood proved to be so strong that the cannonballs fired from the British ships could not destroy the fort, and very few people were injured or killed. The palmetto flag continues to be South Carolina's state flag today.

THE CALIFORNIA 100

The California 100 was a group of approximately 100 men from California who were originally from the East Coast. This patriotic group wished to join the Union forces, but didn't want to be stationed in the West. Because of their desire to be in the thick of the action, they contacted the governor of Massachusetts in the summer of 1862 and requested permission to join a new cavalry regiment being formed in Massachusetts. The governor allowed them to join under the condition that they have their own uniform, flag, and equipment. The group agreed and became officially known as Company A of the Second Massachusetts Cavalry, but was popularly referred to as the "California 100."

The California 100 was so successful that many more volunteers from California signed up to fight for the Union. They were a separate company at first, but later joined forces with the California 100 and

California 100 flag.

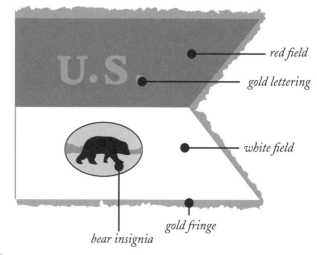

red field

gold lettering

white field

gold fringe

bear insignia

participated in many battles, including the battles of Winchester, Luray, and Cedar Creek. The California 100 carried a flag with a bear on it, and the bear now flies on the California state flag.

HOSPITAL FLAG

Almost every army unit during the Civil War had a flag to signify alliance and unit. Hospital flags were created in order to signal to wounded soldiers that help was nearby. Field hospitals were usually set up in tents behind the battlefield or in a nearby barn; this allowed wounded soldiers to have quick access to medical

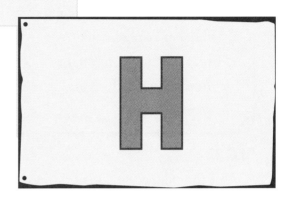

attention, and for doctors and nurses to be close by.

KNOW YOUR SLANG
....
hospital rat—person who fakes illness

The original hospital flag was red; however, this created confusion with the red Confederate flag. Therefore, in 1862, the hospital flag was redesigned as a large, yellow flag, which was later made more distinctive by the addition of a green "H" in the center of the flag. A smaller yellow flag with a green border was used to mark the quickest route to the hospital.

Hospital tents behind Douglas Hospital, Washington, D.C., May 1864.

MAKE YOUR OWN UNION FORT SUMTER FLAG

WHAT YOU'LL NEED

★ **old pillowcase** or other material of any light color

★ **markers, fabric paint, or fabric** in red, white, and blue

★ **paintbrush**

★ **scissors**

★ **pencil/pen**

★ **adhesive/fabric glue**

★ **wooden dowel**

WHAT TO DO

1. Cut the pillowcase so you have one side of it (you can use the other to make a different flag if you'd like).

2. Use the diagram provided to help you sketch and color the features of the flag.* Notice that the stars were in a different configuration than they are today.

3. Attach your flag to the wooden dowel if you choose to do so, otherwise hang it wherever and however you'd like.

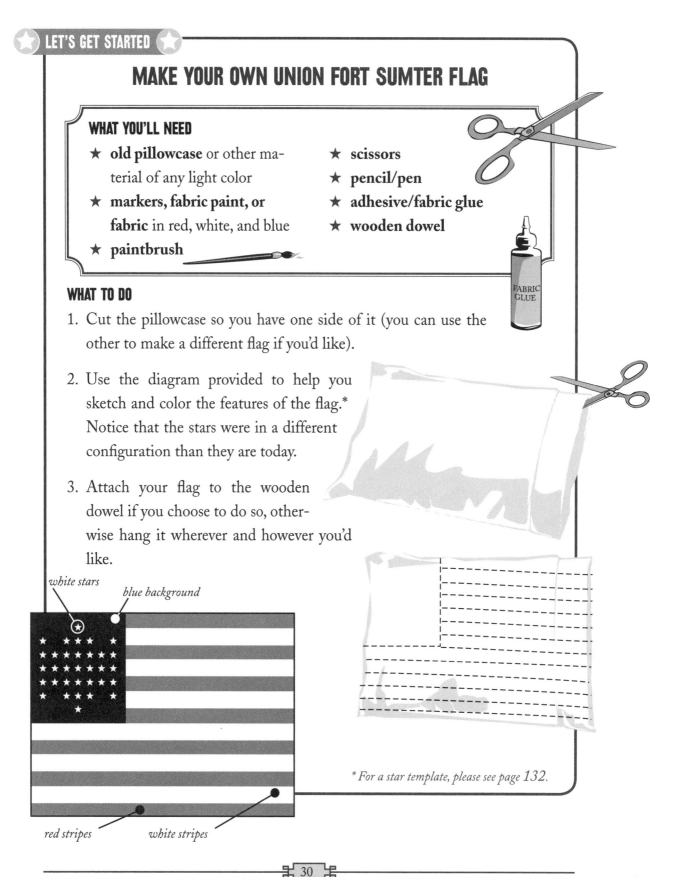

white stars

blue background

red stripes   *white stripes*

* For a star template, please see page 132.

⭐ **LET'S GET STARTED** ⭐

MAKE YOUR OWN PALMETTO FLAG OF SOUTH CAROLINA

WHAT YOU'LL NEED

- ★ **old pillowcase** or other piece of material in any light color
- ★ **dark and light brown material** (felt works well)
- ★ **small piece of red material**
- ★ **wooden dowel**
- ★ **needle and thread** or fabric glue/adhesive
- ★ **scissors**
- ★ **pen/pencil/ruler**

WHAT TO DO

1. Cut the pillowcase so you have one side (save the other side if you'd like to make another flag).

2. Use the dark brown material for the top of the tree and the light brown material for the trunk of the tree. Use the red material for the star. *

3. Using the needle and thread or adhesive, attach the tree and star according to the diagram. You now have a palmetto flag!

4. Use the adhesive or needle and thread to attach the dowel rod; if you decide you don't want to use a dowel, the flag can be hung on a tree, wall, chair, etc.

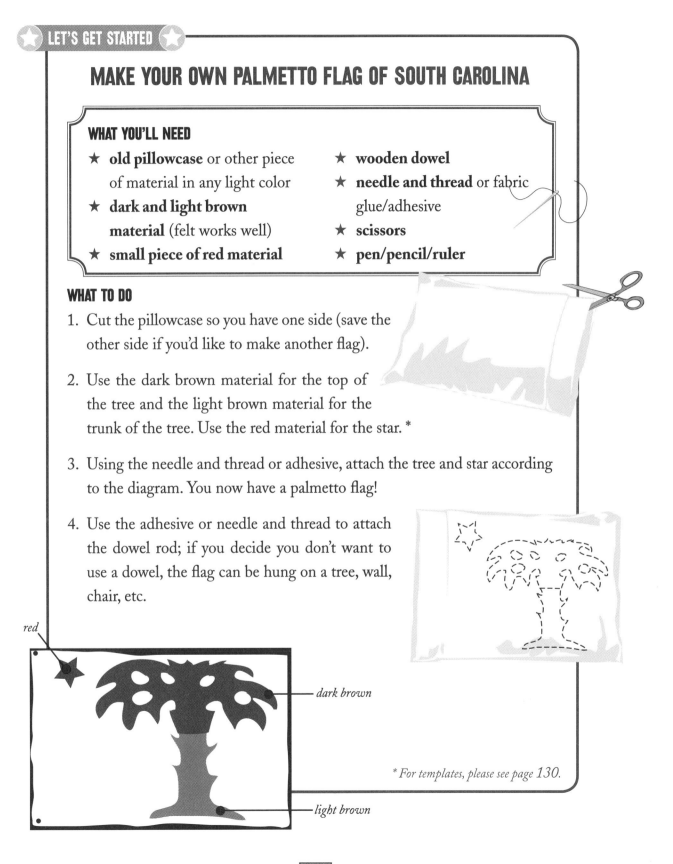

red

dark brown

light brown

For templates, please see page 130.

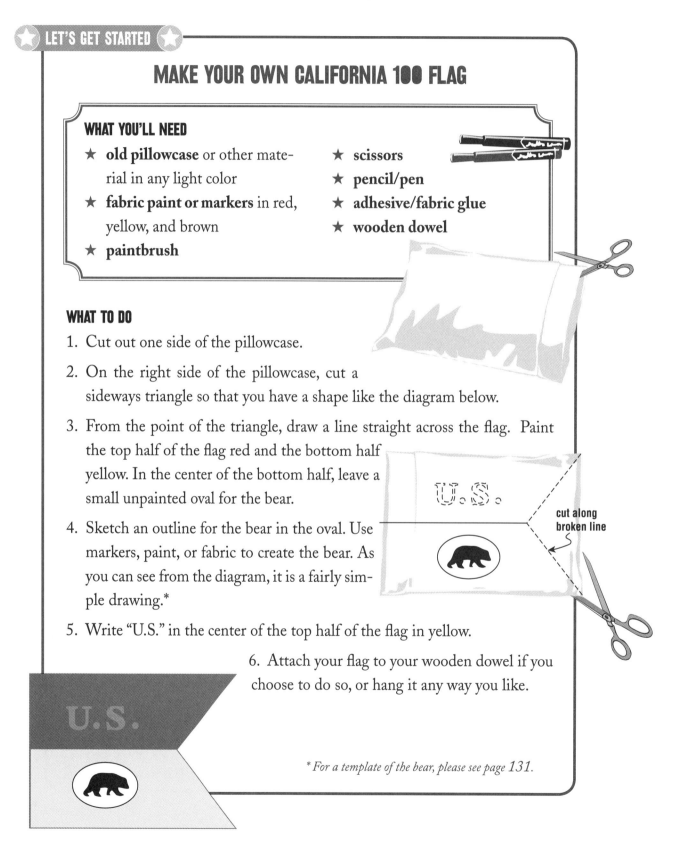

MAKE YOUR OWN CALIFORNIA 100 FLAG

WHAT YOU'LL NEED

★ **old pillowcase** or other material in any light color

★ **fabric paint or markers** in red, yellow, and brown

★ **paintbrush**

★ **scissors**

★ **pencil/pen**

★ **adhesive/fabric glue**

★ **wooden dowel**

WHAT TO DO

1. Cut out one side of the pillowcase.

2. On the right side of the pillowcase, cut a sideways triangle so that you have a shape like the diagram below.

3. From the point of the triangle, draw a line straight across the flag. Paint the top half of the flag red and the bottom half yellow. In the center of the bottom half, leave a small unpainted oval for the bear.

4. Sketch an outline for the bear in the oval. Use markers, paint, or fabric to create the bear. As you can see from the diagram, it is a fairly simple drawing.*

5. Write "U.S." in the center of the top half of the flag in yellow.

6. Attach your flag to your wooden dowel if you choose to do so, or hang it any way you like.

cut along broken line

U. S.

For a template of the bear, please see page 131.

IRONCLAD SHIPS

When Virginia seceded from the Union in 1861, it took with it what would soon be one of the South's most valuable assets: the Union's shipyard in Portsmouth, Virginia. One of the biggest weaknesses the Confederates had was their lack of a naval yard, since almost all of the shipyards were in the Union's northeastern states. The Portsmouth Shipyard was where much of the Union's fleet was repaired, and when Virginia left the Union, everything at the shipyard became the property of the Confederate army, including the *Merrimack*, one of the Union navy's biggest and most powerful ships.

Union sailors burned everything they could before they left the shipyard to the Confederates, including the *Merrimack*, but the ship sank to the river bottom while it was burning, and so it only burned down to the deck. The Confederates dredged the ship up from the river and discovered that it was still usable. They decided to try

something new: to build a ship covered in iron so that cannonballs and shells would bounce off the sides rather than smash them to pieces.

The Confederates built a new structure on top of the ship's deck that had wooden sides two feet thick. On top of that, they lay two layers of 2-inch-thick iron. Ten cannons were placed inside the

USS Merrimack *(1856-1861).*

JOHN ERICSSON, DESIGNER OF THE *MONITOR*

John Ericsson was born in Sweden in 1803 and was a skilled engineer and inventor. He received a patent when living in England for his invention of the screw propeller, which changed the way ships navigated at sea. He also invented a steam engine, rotating turret, and even a deep-sea sounding device.

Ericsson moved to the United States to work for the U.S. navy, and in 1844 designed the USS Princeton, a modern warship propelled by a screw propeller. Unfortunately, when the guns of the ship exploded in front of government naval officials, the secretaries of state and navy were killed. It wasn't Ericsson's fault, but he retired from working for the navy for a long time after that. He was called back into service during the Civil War, and convinced Abraham Lincoln that his odd design for the Monitor would be effective against the Confederate's ironclad ship. He was right, and the rest is history.

ship, their barrels sticking out of narrow openings in the iron-covered sides. One soldier who described the ship said it looked "like the roof of a very big barn belching forth smoke as from a chimney on fire."

The Confederates renamed their new ship the *Virginia* and planned to attack the Union warships in the waters off Norfolk, Virginia, then steam up the Potomac River and attack Washington, D.C.

Meanwhile, Union spies told the Union navy about the ironclad ship the Confederates were building, and the Union set to work on its own ironclad.

CSS Virginia *(1862-1862), wash drawing by Clary Ray, 1898.*

In only 100 days, the Union developed a ship that changed the face of naval warfare forever.

The *Monitor* was unlike any ship ever made: it was described as a cheese box on a raft, and was very slow in the water even though it was a bit faster than the *Virginia*. But what made the *Monitor* so remarkable was its revolving cannon turret. The turret could be turned 360 degrees, so that the two cannons inside could fire in any direction. In contrast, the *Virginia's* cannons could only be fired when the ship was facing its target.

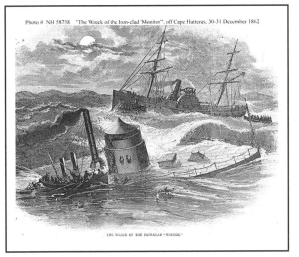

Line engraving published in Harper's Weekly, *1863, depicting USS* Monitor *sinking in a storm off Cape Hatteras on the night of December 30, 1862. A boat is taking off crewmen, and USS* Rhode Island *is in the background.*

On March 8, 1862, the *Virginia* attacked the Union fleet in the waters of Hampton Roads, Virginia, sinking two ships and killing 300 Union sailors. One of the Union ships had 50 cannons, and the Union army had pounded the *Virginia* from the shore, as well. Nothing affected the mighty ironclad, and an urgent message was sent from President Lincoln to northern cities along the coast, warning them that the ship was coming. When night fell, the *Virginia* pulled close to the southern shore, determined to finish off the rest of the fleet the next day.

KNOW YOUR SLANG
....
opening of the ball—units waiting to move into battle

But when the *Virginia* pulled out into open water the next morning to fire on the rest of the Union fleet, the *Monitor* blocked its way. The *Virginia* opened fire on the *Monitor*, and the fire was returned. The two ships pounded each other for more than four hours, with neither winning. Then, with its crew in a state of confusion after the wounding of their captain, the *Monitor* pulled away. The *Virginia* then pulled away, too, assuming that the *Monitor* had given up.

While neither ship actually won the battle, the success of both ships under the assault of so many cannonballs immediately made every wooden warship obsolete.

From this point on, the seas were ruled by ironclad ships and the era of wooden ships was over.

CSS Manassas, *armored ram. Artwork by R. G. Skerrett, 1904.*

CIVIL WAR FACTS & TRIVIA

★ *Both the* **Virginia** *and the* **Monitor** *were destroyed within a year of their historic battle. The Confederate navy destroyed the* **Virginia** *when the Union took over Norfolk, Virginia, in May 1862. They set fire to the ship so the Union navy couldn't use it, and the ship exploded when the fire reached gunpowder stored below deck. The* **Monitor** *was being towed from Virginia to North Carolina to help the Union navy when it was caught in a storm and sank.*

★ *John Ericsson designed every single aspect of the* **Monitor**, *including the first flushing toilets on a ship.*

★ *The cannons on the* **Monitor** *fired solid iron cannonballs that weighed 180 pounds each.*

★ *Both the North and South built several more ironclad ships during the course of the war, including the Confederate ship* **Manassas**, *which looked kind of like a giant egg with a cannon sticking out.*

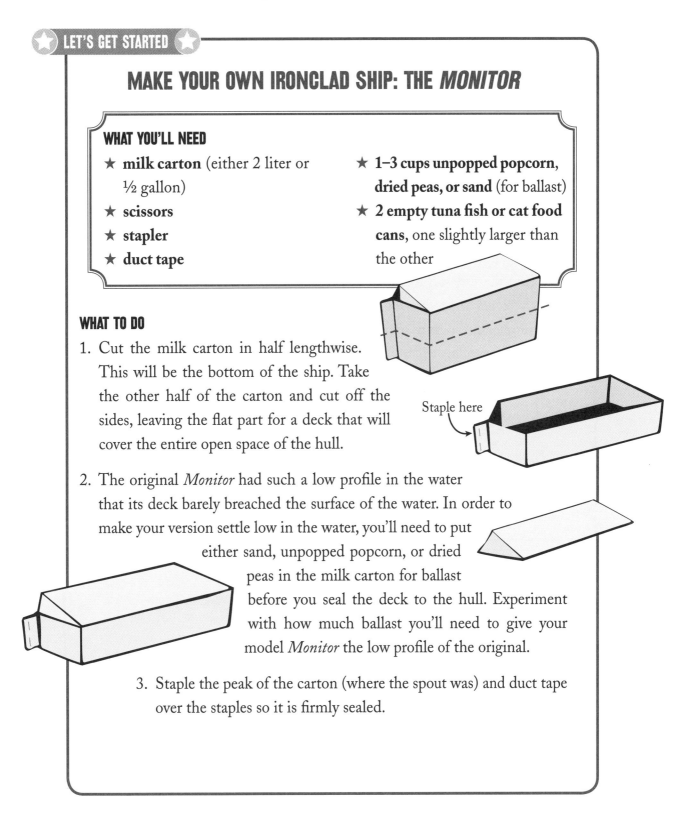

MAKE YOUR OWN IRONCLAD SHIP: THE *MONITOR*

WHAT YOU'LL NEED

★ **milk carton** (either 2 liter or ½ gallon)

★ **scissors**

★ **stapler**

★ **duct tape**

★ **1–3 cups unpopped popcorn, dried peas, or sand** (for ballast)

★ **2 empty tuna fish or cat food cans,** one slightly larger than the other

WHAT TO DO

1. Cut the milk carton in half lengthwise. This will be the bottom of the ship. Take the other half of the carton and cut off the sides, leaving the flat part for a deck that will cover the entire open space of the hull.

Staple here

2. The original *Monitor* had such a low profile in the water that its deck barely breached the surface of the water. In order to make your version settle low in the water, you'll need to put either sand, unpopped popcorn, or dried peas in the milk carton for ballast before you seal the deck to the hull. Experiment with how much ballast you'll need to give your model *Monitor* the low profile of the original.

3. Staple the peak of the carton (where the spout was) and duct tape over the staples so it is firmly sealed.

4. Duct tape the deck onto the hull, and cover the hull in duct tape (this is your "iron" cladding).

5. On the deck, tape the smaller can with the opening face down. This will serve as the base for the *Monitor*'s revolving cannon turret. Then place the larger can over the smaller one so that it can rotate around it. Cover the larger can with duct tape, but make sure the can still rotates. If the top can is much bigger than the bottom one, you can crumple tinfoil and stick it around the smaller can. This will allow the turret to turn around the bottom can but still fit snugly.

USS Monitor, *published in* Harper's Weekly, *March 22, 1862.*

MAKE YOUR OWN IRONCLAD SHIP: THE *VIRGINIA*

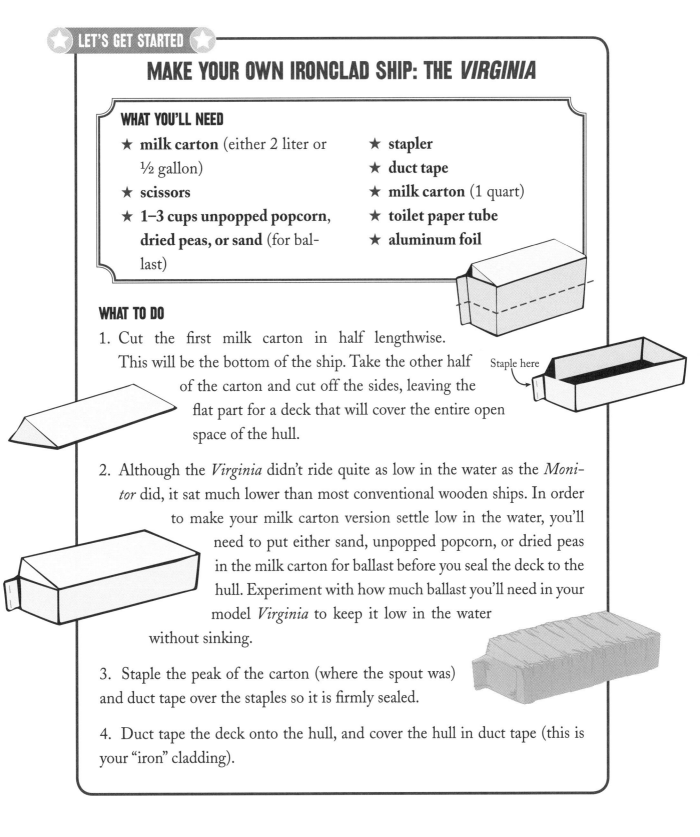

WHAT YOU'LL NEED

- ★ **milk carton** (either 2 liter or ½ gallon)
- ★ **scissors**
- ★ **1–3 cups unpopped popcorn, dried peas, or sand** (for ballast)
- ★ **stapler**
- ★ **duct tape**
- ★ **milk carton** (1 quart)
- ★ **toilet paper tube**
- ★ **aluminum foil**

WHAT TO DO

1. Cut the first milk carton in half lengthwise. This will be the bottom of the ship. Take the other half of the carton and cut off the sides, leaving the flat part for a deck that will cover the entire open space of the hull.

Staple here

2. Although the *Virginia* didn't ride quite as low in the water as the *Monitor* did, it sat much lower than most conventional wooden ships. In order to make your milk carton version settle low in the water, you'll need to put either sand, unpopped popcorn, or dried peas in the milk carton for ballast before you seal the deck to the hull. Experiment with how much ballast you'll need in your model *Virginia* to keep it low in the water without sinking.

3. Staple the peak of the carton (where the spout was) and duct tape over the staples so it is firmly sealed.

4. Duct tape the deck onto the hull, and cover the hull in duct tape (this is your "iron" cladding).

cut along dotted lines

5. Cut both ends off the second milk carton, then cut up the length of one side. You'll have four long panels to work with. Cut off two of the long panels and put them aside. You'll need them later.

fold and crease

6. The other 2-sided panel will be the "barn roof" deckhouse that contained the *Virginia's* mighty cannons. Crease the sides of the outer panels so the deck house sits securely on top of the hull (see diagrams). Before you tape it to the hull, cut out four small rectangles on each side—these would be where the cannon ports on the original *Virginia* would be.

fold and crease again

7. Tape the deckhouse to the hull. Now take the remaining panels from the milk carton and cut two pieces that can fit over the remaining holes in the front and back of the deckhouse. It probably won't fit exactly, but you'll be duct taping over these so it won't matter.

8. Duct tape the deckhouse so that it appears iron clad.

Tape

Tape

9. Finally, create a smokestack by cutting a toilet paper tube about 2 inches long and covering it with foil. Tape this onto the top of the deckhouse.

cut shapes to fill in ends

Now put both the *Monitor* and *Virginia* into the tub and relive the battle of the ironclads.

LEAN-TO SHELTER

Soldiers in both the Union and Confederate armies spent weeks (and sometimes months) in the field, marching from one location to the next. Unless they were lucky enough to camp near a town or a farm that had large buildings, the soldiers usually ended up sleeping outdoors. Not every soldier was able to carry a small tent as part of his supplies, and those who did often found their canvas tents in need of repair. In the Confederate army, in particular, most soldiers below the rank of staff officer didn't have tents at all. Those who did quickly discovered how hard it was to lug a tent with them from place to place, and how quickly poorly made canvas fell apart.

Every soldier quickly learned how to build a simple lean-to shelter. Usually fallen logs or large branches from fallen trees

KNOW YOUR SLANG
snug as a bug—
very comfortable or cozy

DOG TENTS

In old photographs of Civil War camps, you might have seen tent cities, where the ground is covered in A-frame tents in rows that stretch as far as you can see. While this was a common set up for the Union army, it wasn't so for the Confederacy. Most Confederate soldiers were lucky if they had a "shelter half" that they could pair with another soldier's shelter half to make what was known as "dog tents": two shelter halves buttoned together. Soldiers would team up to share dog tents, and they would often write funny sayings on the outside of the tents like, "bulldog pups for sale." Other nicknames for dog tents were dog kennel, picket tent, and pup tent.

were readily available, and when the soldiers were told to set up camp, they scrambled to create a lean-to shelter. They would take two branches about three or four feet in length, and stick them into the ground. Another log or heavy branch was tied to the tops of the branches. Then a few more branches were leaned against the top branch, and the soldiers had the framework for their shelter.

Officers of the One hundred and fourteenth Pennsylvania Infantry playing cards in front of tents, Petersburg, Virginia, August 1864.

Soldiers who had an extra blanket would stretch the blanket across the shelter. Others who did not want to give up their extra blanket (it could get quite cold at night!) or who did not have an extra blanket would simply use moss, leaves, brush, ferns, or whatever was available.

KNOW YOUR SLANG

top rail—first class, the best

possum—a buddy

CIVIL WAR FACTS & TRIVIA

★ *Soldiers who camped out knew they should make their shelters or set up their tents at least 50 yards away from any body of water (such as a river or a lake), because evaporating water tended to add extra chill to the air. Many new soldiers did not believe the story about the evaporating water, and learned the hard way when they set up their tent or lean-to shelter next to the water. By morning they were usually freezing and many became sick.*

★ *One of the few times a Confederate soldier lived in a tent was when he mustered in and went to training camp.*

★ *In 1861 the U.S. army defined the term bivouac as passing the night without shelter, except what could be made with plants and branches.*

MAKE YOUR OWN LEAN-TO SHELTER

WHAT YOU'LL NEED

★ **2 branches** between 3 and 4 feet in length, with a Y at one end of each

★ **5 branches** between 4 and 5 feet in length

★ **old blanket or towel**

★ **heavy cord or kite string**

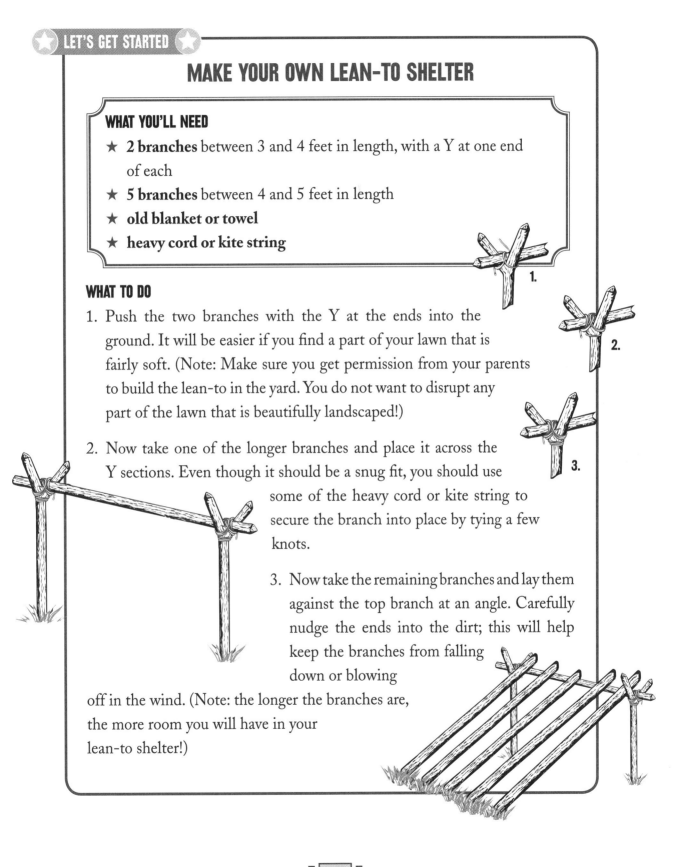

WHAT TO DO

1. Push the two branches with the Y at the ends into the ground. It will be easier if you find a part of your lawn that is fairly soft. (Note: Make sure you get permission from your parents to build the lean-to in the yard. You do not want to disrupt any part of the lawn that is beautifully landscaped!)

2. Now take one of the longer branches and place it across the Y sections. Even though it should be a snug fit, you should use some of the heavy cord or kite string to secure the branch into place by tying a few knots.

3. Now take the remaining branches and lay them against the top branch at an angle. Carefully nudge the ends into the dirt; this will help keep the branches from falling down or blowing off in the wind. (Note: the longer the branches are, the more room you will have in your lean-to shelter!)

4. Drape the blanket or towel over the branches.

5. Sit inside your lean-to shelter and try to imagine what life was like for the Civil War soldiers. It's also fun to sleep out in your shelter.

Variations to the outdoor lean-to:

If you don't have access to a backyard full of branches, you can use any sort of stick or pole that you can find. For instance, you could use broom or rake handles, ski poles, or garden stakes. You could build your lean-to up against the wall of a building. If you decide to do this, you may need some other stabilizing sticks in order to hold it up. If you need to build your lean-to inside, build it up against a bed, couch, or other object that is a good height. In both of these cases, be careful that the lean-to is stable and that it won't fall on top of you if you're under it. Do this by using rope or other material to stabilize your lean-to, making it solid enough for you to spend time in it!

SHELTERS OF ALL KINDS

Most Union soldiers were issued shelter halfs, which were, literally, half a shelter. Shelter halfs were pieces of canvas cloth with buttons. Two halves of the shelter could be buttoned together to make a complete tent. Sometimes, three or four soldiers would button their shelter halves together to create a larger tent structure.

A-frame tents, also known as wedge tents, were also used during the first year or so of the Civil War, but were heavy and bulky and had to be carried by wagon. A-frame tents were discontinued early in the war, since they were just too impractical for field use.

During the winter months, most of the fighting ceased, and soldiers built log huts about five feet tall, using their tents as roofs. They would build fireplaces on one end of the log hut, using sticks or bricks, with a barrel for a chimney.

PADDLEWHEELERS AND HOSPITAL SHIPS

When Robert Fulton designed the first working steamboat in 1807, he probably didn't realize that his invention would lead to one of the most interesting innovations of the Civil War. Steamboats revolutionized river travel during the 1800s: for the first time, people were able to travel up and down America's mighty waterways under motorized power, rather than relying on muscle or the wind. Steamboats became the fastest and most efficient way to transport people and goods up and down the United States rivers. St. Louis, Missouri, a major port on the Mississippi River, had more than 3,000 steamboat arrivals in 1850 alone.

When the Civil War erupted, control of the country's rivers became more important than ever. Both the Confederate and Union armies had flotillas of boats they used as floating barracks, supply ships, and gunboats for fighting against artillery units in-

CONTRABANDS TO FREEDOM

For many runaway slaves in the South, the best chance for freedom was to get on board a Union boat like Red Rover *as it steamed up or down the Mississippi River. These slaves were called "contraband," and many ships hired them to serve as cabin boys, carpenters, laborers, cooks, stewards, crewman, and nurses. Working on board* Red Rover *had many advantages, one being the pay: the ship's records show that several chambermaids were paid $20 a month for their work. In comparison, the base pay for infantrymen in the Union army was only $13 a month.*

Medical supply boat Planter *at General Hospital wharf on the Appomattox River.*

stalled on the banks above key river locations. One such floating supply ship was *Red Rover*.

The Confederate paddlewheeler *Red Rover* was on the Mississippi River near St. Louis when it was captured by a Union gunboat. The Confederates tried to sink *Red Rover* to put it out of use, but the Union was able to dredge it and repair it for service. And although the Union was desperate for more gunboats to patrol the Mississippi and its tributaries, it decided to try something new with the *Red Rover*: the army refitted *Red Rover* as a floating hospital.

Transporting wounded soldiers by boat was nothing new for either army, but it was usually a pretty terrible experience for soldiers who were already

PADDLEWHEELERS—PROS AND CONS

One reason paddlewheelers became so prevalent during the 1800s was that they were ideally suited to river travel: most paddleboats had a draft of no more than 6 or 7 feet, and some had as few as 4 feet, which meant they were able to steam up and down the wide, shallow rivers of the American West much better than any deep-hulled boats. The problem with them, however, was that their flat hulls were very difficult to maneuver if the weather or water got rough, since steering a paddlewheeler was very much like steering a giant box.

Paddlewheeler.

in bad shape: the boats were loud, dirty, and rarely had the supplies or personnel necessary to treat illness or injury. Transport ships usually picked up wounded soldiers at the port closest to the battle, brought them to the nearest friendly hospital, and dropped them off. Not a lot of medicine was being practiced on these ships, and the conditions were difficult.

Neither the Union nor Confederacy had ever created a complete hospital aboard a steamship before, and *Red Rover* was refitted with innovations never before found on a ship, all designed to help the sick and wounded. It had separate operating and amputation rooms, and the windows were covered with gauze to keep cinders and smoke from the smokestacks away from the patients. Rooms at the back of the ship had open walls to allow for better air circulation, and patients who had contagious

KNOW YOUR SLANG

sawbones—surgeon

diseases were put in these, as well as on several separate floating barges attached to the back of the ship. This helped keep the spread of very contagious diseases, such as measles and typhus, from infecting everyone on board. *Red Rover* also carried enough medical and food supplies for two hundred patients and the entire crew for up to

Acting Assistant Surgeon George Hopkins from the USS Red Rover.

three months—everything the hospital staff needed was on board, making the ship completely self-sufficient if it needed to be.

And while *Red Rover* was remarkable as the first complete floating hospital, what was more amazing was her crew: it consisted not only of the first women serving in the U.S. armed forces, but also the first African-American women hired by either side.

Red Rover's reputation as a hospital with conveniences, comfortable accommodations, and very caring medical staff grew quickly; so quickly, in fact, that fleet commander Charles Henry Davis had to issue an order to limit the number of patients being sent to the ship—it seemed like every sick or injured soldier wanted to be cared for on *Red Rover*. The order apparently didn't work all the time, since the ship's log shows that many patients came on without papers, or simply under the verbal approval of particular doctors or high-ranking officials.

Red Rover transported and cared for soldiers throughout the war, shuttling from port to port on the Mississippi River. Most of its hospital duties came to an end after the Battle of Vicksburg in 1863, which gave the Union control over most of the waterways and marked the end of most of the river action on the western front. For the rest of the war, *Red Rover* was primarily used to transport supplies.

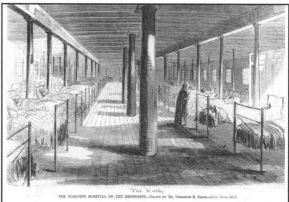

Line engraving after a drawing by Theodore R. Davis, published in Harper's Weekly, *January–June 1863, depicting a scene in the hospital ward aboard* Red Rover.

CIVIL WAR FACTS & TRIVIA

★ *The women who served as nurses on* **Red Rover** *are credited with officially being the first women to serve on board a naval vessel. In most accounts, the nuns who served on* **Red Rover** *are given the credit for being the first U.S. naval nurses, even though the ship's records show that the contraband women were hired outright after being welcomed on board, making them the first paid women naval employees.*

★ *From the end of the Civil War to 1908, women were not allowed to serve in the navy.*

★ *The majority of* **Red Rover's** *crew was African-American: at one point, black sailors and crew outnumbered white crew by two to one. It wasn't until 1865 that white crewmen outnumbered black crewmen.*

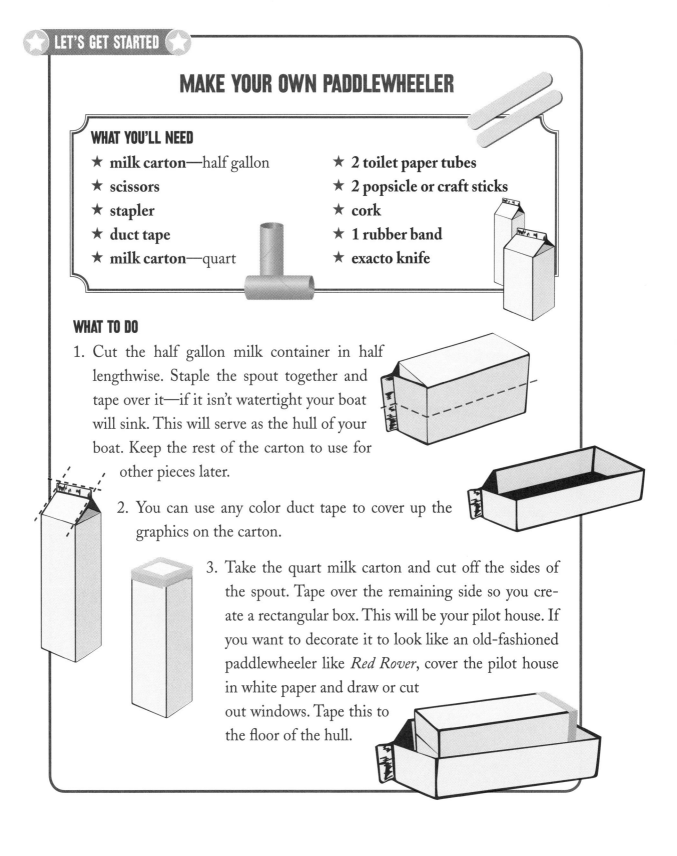

MAKE YOUR OWN PADDLEWHEELER

WHAT YOU'LL NEED

- ★ **milk carton**—half gallon
- ★ **scissors**
- ★ **stapler**
- ★ **duct tape**
- ★ **milk carton**—quart
- ★ **2 toilet paper tubes**
- ★ **2 popsicle or craft sticks**
- ★ **cork**
- ★ **1 rubber band**
- ★ **exacto knife**

WHAT TO DO

1. Cut the half gallon milk container in half lengthwise. Staple the spout together and tape over it—if it isn't watertight your boat will sink. This will serve as the hull of your boat. Keep the rest of the carton to use for other pieces later.

2. You can use any color duct tape to cover up the graphics on the carton.

3. Take the quart milk carton and cut off the sides of the spout. Tape over the remaining side so you create a rectangular box. This will be your pilot house. If you want to decorate it to look like an old-fashioned paddlewheeler like *Red Rover*, cover the pilot house in white paper and draw or cut out windows. Tape this to the floor of the hull.

4. Decorate the toilet paper tubes to look like smoke-stacks (white on the bottom with a black rim around the top). Tape the toilet paper tubes on each end of the pilot house.

5. To make the paddle, tape one popsicle stick to each side of the hull of your ship, making sure that more than half of the stick is protruding beyond the back end of the boat. You may want to put tape on both the outside of the boat and inside the hull to reinforce where the popsicle sticks attach to the sides of the boat.

6. Take the cork and make four slits the length of the cork, equal distances apart. This will hold your paddle blades and the rubber band.

7. Cut two paddle blades from a piece of leftover milk carton—the stiffer the blades are, the better, so try to cut them from the bottom of the carton. The blades will need to be the same length as the cork, and wide enough to catch water—but make sure they aren't so wide that they will hit the back of your boat when you attach the paddlewheel to the sticks.

8. Slide the blades into two opposite slits on the cork. Slide the rubber band firmly into the other slits as shown and then stretch the rubber band around the outside of the popsicle sticks. You may need to duct tape the rubber band into the cork to keep it in place.

9. From the remaining half of the milk carton, cut out two half-circles that are the same length as the popsicle sticks. Decorate the plain side of these with the name of your ship. Tape these over the popsicle sticks with the flat side facing the water. Make sure you can still wind the cork paddlewheel and that the paddlewheel moves freely.

10. Place your ship in the water, wind up the paddlewheel, and let her go.*

*You may find that the boat is easier to maneuver with a little weight, or ballast, in the bottom.

Red Rover, *the Navy's first hospital ship, was a side wheel steamer built in 1859.*

PERISCOPES

One of the biggest innovations of the Civil War was a change in how war was waged. When the war began, everyone prepared to fight using the same methods that had been used in the past, from the Napoleonic wars and American Revolution to the War of 1812. Weapons in past wars had been so inaccurate and slow to reload that most of the fighting was very close. Armies marched toward each other in formation, then each set up two lines of fighters, the first line kneeling to shoot and the second line standing and shooting over the front line.

KNOW YOUR SLANG
....
picket—a guard or guard duty

But what soldiers discovered during the Civil War was that while the tactics remained the same, the weapons had changed. Weapons like the Gatling gun, which fired 250 rounds a minute from six barrels, repeating rifles, breech-loading cannons, and other weapons were not only more accurate, they shot farther and were much easier and faster to reload. These weapons were so different from what had been used in the past that, in the four years from the start of the Civil War at Fort Sumter to Robert E. Lee's surrender at Appomattox Court House, the entire theory for how to fight a war changed.

Soldiers in the trenches, Petersburg, Virginia. 1865.

At the beginning of the war, soldiers would mass together and charge the enemy, ready for close, hand-to-hand fighting. But unlike earlier wars, when, as Ulysses S. Grant said, "A man might fire at you all day without you finding it out," soldiers found that charging toward an enemy whose guns could reload quickly and shoot hundreds of rounds a minute with great accuracy from half a mile away meant that men were being killed and injured in shocking numbers.

So, by the later battles of the war, rather than quick, close, and decisive victories, the Union and Confederate

The first Federal wagons moving into Petersburg.

THE SIEGE OF PETERSBURG

The most famous Civil War battle where siege-style method of warfare was used was in the city of Petersburg, Virginia.

armies were stuck in what is known as siege warfare: battles that lasted for long stretches—sometimes months at a time—where armies dug and stayed in trenches, didn't engage in active fighting very often, and waited out their enemy. The Siege of Petersburg, Virginia, for example, took 10 months. Lots of soldiers, especially Southern soldiers defending the city, dug and then lived in trenches.

This style of fighting called for new ways of keeping track of the enemy. Soldiers needed a way to see what their enemies were doing while they sat in their trenches, without having to pop up and potentially get their heads shot off. The best tool for this was the periscope.

Union soldiers at Appomattox Court House.

Part of the trench system outside Petersburg, Virginia.

Thomas Doughty, a naval officer for the Union, is given credit for inventing the periscope for his gunship, the USS *Osage*. Gunners on the ship couldn't see the high banks of Louisiana's Red River out of the peepholes of the ship, and they couldn't risk going on deck, so Doughty used his periscope to see above the turret and direct his guns.

The periscope quickly became a useful tool for soldiers in the trenches as well as on gunships, helping them to see what was going on outside the trenches without being harmed in the process.

KNOW YOUR SLANG

bombproof—an underground shelter; also an officer or soldier who never went to the front

hornets—bullets

CIVIL WAR FACTS & TRIVIA

★ *During the Siege of Petersburg, soldiers dug trenches about 3 feet deep and 6 to 8 feet wide. In front of these trenches were small rifle pits, which were large enough for two riflemen. Trenches were sometimes big enough to hold wagons.*

★ *During long battles or sieges, soldiers would sleep in small shelters built of earth and sandbags, or in caves dug in the trenches. These shelters were usually very small and uncomfortable, but were bulletproof and protected soldiers overnight.*

★ *The trench lines dug during the Seige of Petersburg ran for 53 miles. By the end of the siege, there were 61,000 Union casualties and 38,000 Confederate casualties.*

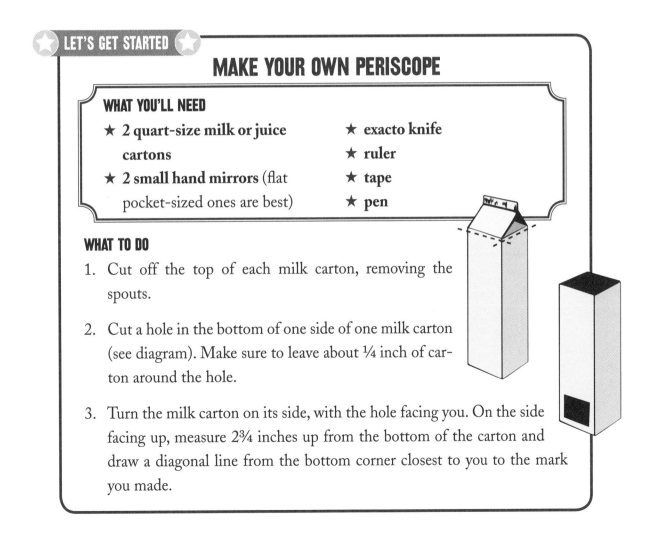

LET'S GET STARTED

MAKE YOUR OWN PERISCOPE

WHAT YOU'LL NEED

★ **2 quart-size milk or juice cartons**

★ **2 small hand mirrors** (flat pocket-sized ones are best)

★ **exacto knife**

★ **ruler**

★ **tape**

★ **pen**

WHAT TO DO

1. Cut off the top of each milk carton, removing the spouts.

2. Cut a hole in the bottom of one side of one milk carton (see diagram). Make sure to leave about ¼ inch of carton around the hole.

3. Turn the milk carton on its side, with the hole facing you. On the side facing up, measure 2¾ inches up from the bottom of the carton and draw a diagonal line from the bottom corner closest to you to the mark you made.

2¾ inches

4. Use the exacto knife to cut a slit on that line, but don't cut all the way to the edge of the carton—this is where you will place your mirror, and it works best if the mirror fits in the slot snugly.

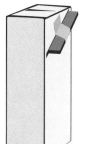

mirror side

5. Slide your mirror into the cut so that the mirror faces the hole in the carton. Hold it up and look through the hole at the mirror. You should be able to see out the top of the milk carton. If you can't, adjust the mirror so that you have a clear view out of the top of the milk carton. Tape the mirror loosely in place .

6. Repeat the above steps with the other milk carton.

7. Stand one carton on the table, with the hole facing you. Put the other carton on the table upside down, with the mirror on the top and the hole facing away from you.

8. Put the carton with the hole facing away from you on top of the one with the hole facing you. You should be able to squeeze the top carton slightly into the bottom one. Tape these together.

9 Look through the bottom hole. You should be able to see out of the top milk carton, which will be about a foot higher than your normal field of vision. Imagine you are in a trench with bullets whizzing over your head. Sticking a periscope up would be a lot safer than sticking your head out.

SOLDIERS' FOOD

Hardtack, aslo known as sheet iron crackers.

During the war, soldiers were given "rations" of food; this means that they received a certain amount every week or month, and every soldier was given the same amount. Staple foods included a cracker-like biscuit called hardtack, dried or salted beef or pork, coffee, and dried vegetables and fruit. They also received flour or cornmeal as well as sugar, beans, tea, salt, soap, and potatoes. It was simple food, and although soldiers seemed to get enough calories to sustain themselves, the food was deficient in certain required nutrients, such as vitamin C. This resulted in a disease called scurvy, which could cause death and weaken an army. Sometimes, soldiers would write home and request that a certain food or drink be sent to them, but this could only occur if a soldier was going to be at camp for an extended period of time. There were also people called sutlers who were authorized to travel to army camps and sell foods that weren't issued to soldiers through rations, such as milk or fresh vegetables. However, this food was often too expensive for soldiers, and they settled for what they had.

Food rations were uncooked, so it was up to the soldiers to prepare their own meals. This

Noncommissioned officers dining out.

meant that they had to start a fire and find water if it wasn't given to them, which often created a challenge. Some soldiers cooked and ate their food together, combining rations. This was called a mess, and the soldiers who cooked together referred to each other as "messmates." Some soldiers preferred to cook their food alone, keeping their rations separate.

Food distribution was organized by the Commissary Department of both the Confederate and Union armies. The Commissary Department was responsible for purchasing the food, transporting it to the troops, and keeping the food from going bad in the process. Sometimes a herd of cattle would move with the army (herded by soldiers or commissary workers), providing fresh meat, but most of the time meat was smoked or salted to keep it from spoiling, and fruits and vegetables were dehydrated. Hardtack kept well unless it got wet: then, mold, weevils, or maggots would make hardtack their home. When this happened, soldiers would drop the hardtack into a steaming cup of coffee, killing the bugs and making them float to the top. They would then skim the bugs off the surface of the coffee, and be left with coffee and softened bread.

KNOW YOUR SLANG

vittles—*food or rations*

bread basket—*stomach*

grab a root—*have dinner or a potato*

Commissary depot with supply train wagons, Cedar Level, Virginia.

Soldiers in both the North and the South suffered from food shortages—supply lines were often interrupted, soldiers were often marching from location to location faster than their supplies could keep up, and in many cases, the armies just couldn't provide enough food for all of the men fighting. Soldiers on both sides foraged for food in the countryside, which took livestock and crops away from the civilians, leaving them hungry, as well. Foraging, or living off the land (which in most cases meant stealing from civilians), became such a problem that it was outlawed and soldiers caught foraging were arrested.

CIVIL WAR FACTS & TRIVIA

★ *One of the most popular dishes for soldiers (when they could get it) was baked beans. It was so popular that three songs about baked beans were written during the war, and Robert E. Lee is reported to have said about his troops, "All I would have to do to keep them happy is to give them beans three times every day."*

★ *Coffee was considered perhaps the most important food for Northern armies, while tobacco was treasured by Southern armies. On rare occasions, Union and Confederate soldiers met on picket lines and traded these items with one another, since tobacco was not included in Northern rations and coffee became very rare in Southern rations.*

KNOW YOUR SLANG

picket line—the line between Confederate and Union soldiers on the battlefield

★ *Before the Civil War began, a Southern family would spend about $6–7 per month on food—this included staples, as well as anything they didn't grow themselves. By 1864, however, groceries cost that same family about $400 per month. The scarcity and expense of food caused malnourishment in many families.*

★ *If soldiers were lucky, they would receive food such as vacuum-packed meat or vegetables in tin cans or jars, as well as condensed milk. These packaging processes had just been invented and allowed food to endure long travel distances and stay "fresh" over long periods of time.*

MAKE YOUR OWN UNION HARDTACK

Here are recipes that will help you eat like a Union or Confederate soldier.

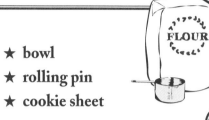

WHAT YOU'LL NEED

- ★ 2 cups of flour
- ★ ½ to ¾ cup water
- ★ salt (5–6 pinches)
- ★ bowl
- ★ rolling pin
- ★ cookie sheet

WHAT TO DO

1. Mix all ingredients together. Make sure you add enough flour so that the dough is no longer sticky, but be careful not to make it too dry. Knead the dough a few times. During the war, hardtack was about half an inch thick, so when you're rolling the dough, aim for this thickness. It is easiest to roll the dough directly on an ungreased cookie sheet. Bake at 350 degrees for about 30 minutes.

2. Remove the dough from the oven, cut the large square into smaller three-by-three-inch squares. Poke 16 evenly spaced holes in each square. Flip, return to the oven, and bake for another 30 minutes. Turn the oven off, and allow the hardtack to cool in the oven with the door closed. Allow to completely cool, and then enjoy!

Variation: Soldiers often soaked their hardtack in leftover water from boiling their meat. This softened the hardtack, and also gave it some flavor. They would then fry the softened hardtack in pork grease. The end result tasted something like a crouton and was called "skillygallee."

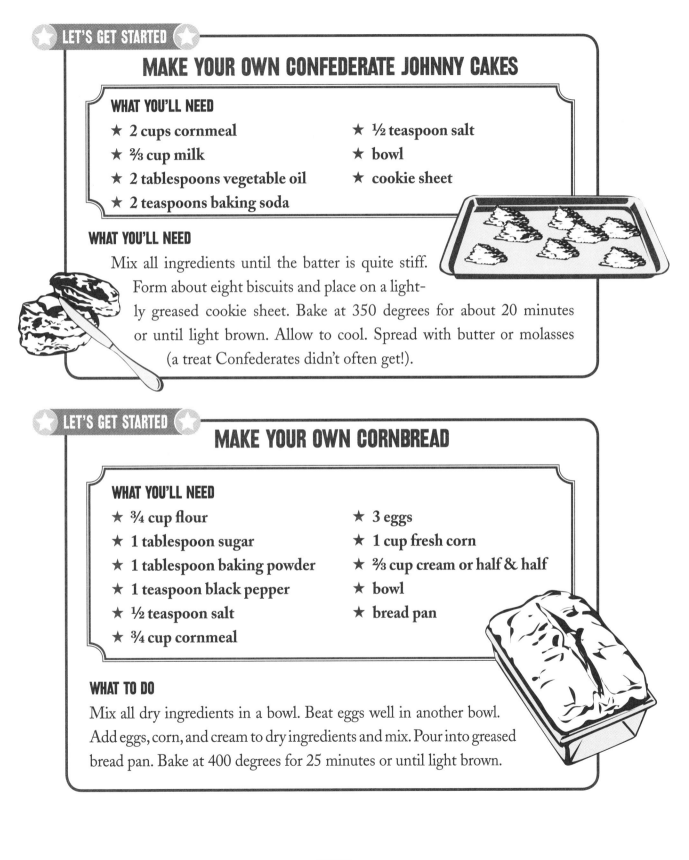

LET'S GET STARTED

MAKE YOUR OWN CONFEDERATE JOHNNY CAKES

WHAT YOU'LL NEED

- ★ 2 cups cornmeal
- ★ ⅔ cup milk
- ★ 2 tablespoons vegetable oil
- ★ 2 teaspoons baking soda
- ★ ½ teaspoon salt
- ★ bowl
- ★ cookie sheet

WHAT YOU'LL NEED

Mix all ingredients until the batter is quite stiff. Form about eight biscuits and place on a lightly greased cookie sheet. Bake at 350 degrees for about 20 minutes or until light brown. Allow to cool. Spread with butter or molasses (a treat Confederates didn't often get!).

LET'S GET STARTED

MAKE YOUR OWN CORNBREAD

WHAT YOU'LL NEED

- ★ ¾ cup flour
- ★ 1 tablespoon sugar
- ★ 1 tablespoon baking powder
- ★ 1 teaspoon black pepper
- ★ ½ teaspoon salt
- ★ ¾ cup cornmeal
- ★ 3 eggs
- ★ 1 cup fresh corn
- ★ ⅔ cup cream or half & half
- ★ bowl
- ★ bread pan

WHAT TO DO

Mix all dry ingredients in a bowl. Beat eggs well in another bowl. Add eggs, corn, and cream to dry ingredients and mix. Pour into greased bread pan. Bake at 400 degrees for 25 minutes or until light brown.

TELEGRAPH AND MORSE CODE

Many historians consider the Civil War the first modern war not only because of innovations in weapons and battle tactics, but also because of advances in communication. In 1844, Samuel Morse, a young New York inventor and successful painter, perfected a way to send coded messages from one location to another using an electromagnetic current, creating the first reliable telegraph. Morse also invented a code using a series of dots and dashes (what we now know as Morse code) to send messages along the current. Telegraph operators translated the dots and dashes, which were punched into a piece of paper with an automatic stylus, into English words. Eventually, telegraph operators became so good at deciphering the code that they were able to translate messages immediately as they came through the lines.

Samuel Morse

KNOW YOUR SLANG
jawings—talking

Samuel Morse first planned to create an underground telegraph system by burying the telegraph wire in pipes running from Washington, D.C., to Baltimore, Maryland, and he was awarded $30,000 by Congress to put

> *The best way to learn Morse code is to memorize the sounds each letter makes. Dots sound like "dit." Dashes sound like "dah." The letters "SOS," the famous plea to "save our ship," sounds like this: "dit dit dit, dah dah dah, dit dit dit."*

WHO WERE THEY?

According to the 1860 census, about 2,000 people were employed as telegraph workers in the year just prior to the start of the Civil War. Most were men, but as many as 200 women also worked as telegraphers. One of the first women telegraphers was Sarah G. Bagley, a known women's rights activist and newspaper editor. Her participation helped make telegraphy the first technical career open to women. The telegraph became important for communication during the war, and military telegraphers were vital in relaying important military information. These workers were both men and women. Despite their important contribution to the war effort the living and working conditions for military telegraphers were miserable. Furthermore, they did not receive pay or pension as normal soldiers did, and they often were placed in highly dangerous zones without adequate protection. Many of them died of disease or injury during the war.

Women were an important part of the work force of the early telegraphs.

his project into action. These 40 miles of telegraph line were intended to allow Morse to demonstrate his new form of communication, but problems arose. The wire bought for the project was faulty and the project was running out of time and money. The fastest and cheapest alternative was to string the lines on trees and poles from Baltimore to Washington, and that's how telegraph (and later telephone) poles and wires became part of the American landscape. On May 24, 1844, Morse transmitted the words "what God hath wrought" from the office of the Supreme Court in Washington, D.C., to a train station in Baltimore—the first-ever electronic message.

Teams constructing telegraph lines, April 1864.

The telegraph would forever change communication. By 1861, telegraph lines ran from coast to coast, owned mostly by the railroads, which put up lines next to the tracks. Transmitting messages via telegraph became a standard method of communication.

The telegraph also had a huge impact on how the Civil War was fought and won. In the Revolutionary War and the War of 1812, armies relied on messages delivered on foot or horseback—communication depended on whether the messenger made it to the destination, whether he could find the people he needed to deliver the message to, and how quickly he could do it. As a result, changes in battle strategy were very slow. But in the Civil War, both sides used telegraph teams to relay information from one place to another in a matter of minutes. For the first time, armies were able to communicate with each other over long distances very quickly and efficiently, which meant that they could make important battlefield decisions immediately.

Telegraph battery wagon.

CIVIL WAR FACTS & TRIVIA

Field telegraph station in Virginia.

★ *The telegraph was an important tool for communication on the battlefield, but it was also an important tool for spies: both sides intercepted telegraphed messages in attempts to learn each others' battle plans.*

★ *More than 15,000 miles of telegraph lines were strung for use by both Union and Confederate armies during the Civil War.*

★ *The Telegraph Service wasn't part of either the Union or Confederate army, and the telegraph operators were actually civilians working for the Quartermasters Department. More than 300 telegraph operators died during the Civil War, and their families received no pension or other support from the government.*

★ *President Lincoln did not have immediate access to telegraph wires, as they didn't go directly to the White House. He had to cross the street to a telegraph office to check messages.*

MORSE CODE ALPHABET

A	.-	L	.-..	W	.--	6	-....
B	--...	M	--	X	-..-	7	--...
C	-.-.	N	-.	Y	-.--	8	---..
D	-..	O	---	Z	--..	9	----.
E	.	P	.--.	**NUMBERS**		**FULL STOP**	
F	..-.	Q	--.-	0	-----		.-.-.-
G	--.	R	.-.	1	.----		
H	....	S	...	2	..---	**COMMA**	
I	..	T	-	3	...--		--..--
J	.---	U	..-	4	....-		
K	-.-	V	...-	5	.....	**QUERY**	..--..

CIVIL WAR BALLOONS

Both the Union and Confederate armies conducted aerial reconnaissance: they tried to spy on each other's armies from the air. How did it work? By balloon.

Thaddeus Lowe observing the battle from his balloon Intrepid, *Fair Oaks, Virginia.*

The most famous balloonist from the Civil War was Thaddeus Lowe. Lowe realized that hot air balloons would be perfect vehicles for spying on the Confederate positions. He convinced President Lincoln to establish a Balloon Corps and built the first Union balloon. Named The Union, *this balloon was filled with hydrogen and went up 1,000 feet over Washington, D.C, still tethered to the ground. Lowe was able to spy on Confederate troops more than three miles away, and telegraphed information to the troops below. Union troops were then able to fire on the Confederates without even seeing where they were from the ground. This was such a successful mission that Lowe was given the money to build six more balloons for the Balloon Corps.*

The Confederate army also had a very small balloon corps, led by Captain John Bryan. The Confederates built two hydrogen balloons, but one never made it into the sky and the other was used for about a year over the skies of Richmond before it escaped in a high wind and was captured by the Union.

Although balloons gave both the Union and Confederate armies information about each other that they couldn't have received any other way, it turned out that balloon reconnaissance wasn't worth the cost or time involved to build and manage them, or the risk. The Union Balloon Corps was disbanded in 1863, and the Confederates lost their last balloon around that same time.

MAKE YOUR OWN TELEGRAPH

WHAT YOU'LL NEED

★ **2 pieces of wood**, anywhere from 4 to 6 inches long and 2 to 3 inches wide. Scrap wood is great.

★ **9 small wood screws or nails**

★ **4 flat strips of metal** with three of them about 4 inches long. One should be about 7 inches long and MUST be iron-bearing or "ferrous" metal (metal that is attracted by a magnet). The easiest metal to use is metal strapping—strips of metal with holes pre-drilled—which you can buy at any hardware store.

★ **2 C or 2 D batteries**

★ **large rubber band**

★ **2 large iron nails** (about 2 to 3 inches long)

★ **20 feet or more of INSULATED solid wire**, about 1/64 inch or less in diameter—this is easy to find at hardware stores and is very inexpensive.

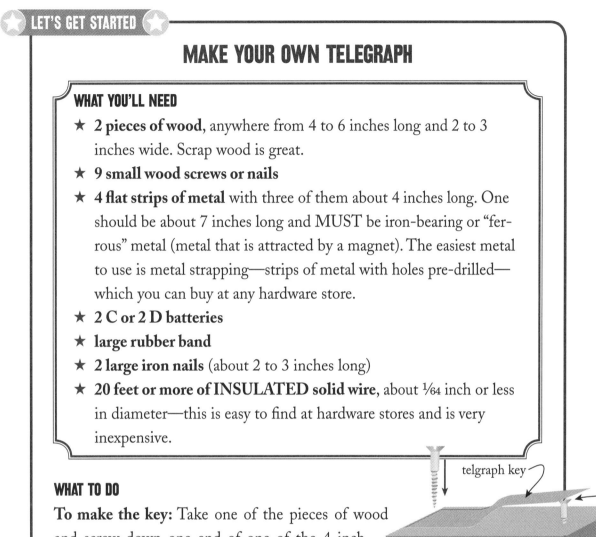

telgraph key

space

WHAT TO DO

To make the key: Take one of the pieces of wood and screw down one end of one of the 4-inch-long pieces of metal strapping. Screw another wood screw directly into the wood at the other end of the block so the bent strapping (as shown) will make a connection with the screw if you push down on it. This will be your telegraph key. The key should not touch the screw unless you push down on it.

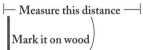

├─ Measure this distance ─┤

Mark it on wood

To make the battery holder: Measure the length of the two batteries placed end to end, and mark the length on the second piece of wood. Screw two of the 4-inch strips of strapping to the wood at either end of the mark so the strapping will touch the connections on the bottoms or, "ends" of the batteries. Place the batteries in the holder, and put the rubber band around both pieces of metal strapping as shown above. This will keep the strapping pressed against the battery contacts.

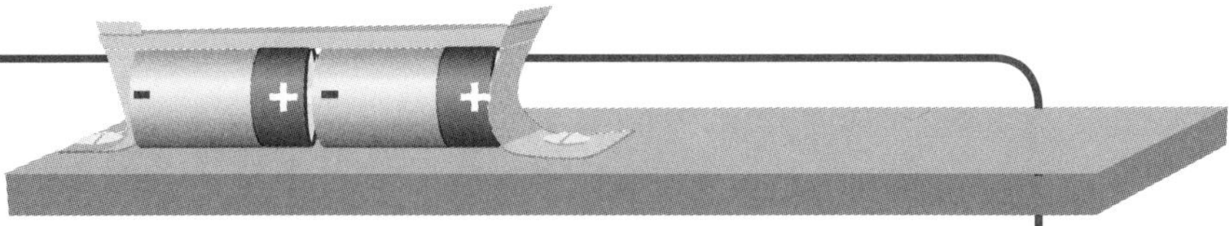

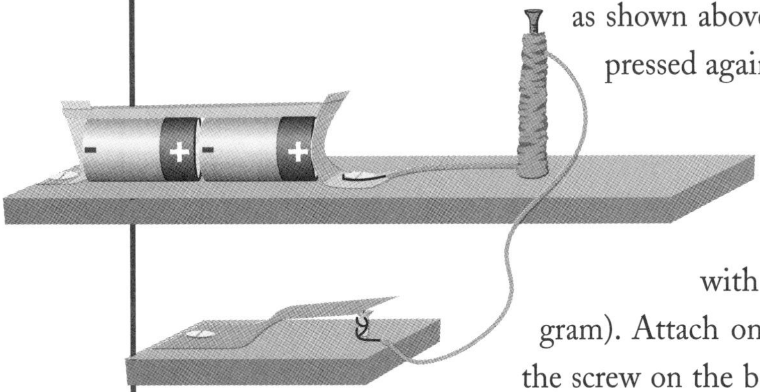

To make the sounder: Nail one of the long iron nails into the second piece of wood with the battery holder (see diagram). Attach one end of the insulated wire to the screw on the battery holder. Wind about 100 turns of the insulated wire around the nail, and attach the other end of the wire to the screw under the telegraph key on the other piece of wood.

Take the 7-inch-long piece of metal strapping and screw it to the piece of wood so that you can bend it up and over the long nail with the insulated wire wound around it. When the battery is connected, the electric current will pass through the wire coiled around the iron nail and will make the nail into an electromagnet. It will pull the piece of bent metal down onto it, making a clicking sound. Make sure the metal is bent close enough to the nail so it will connect when the battery is connected.

Tuck metal strap under head of nail

Second nail

space

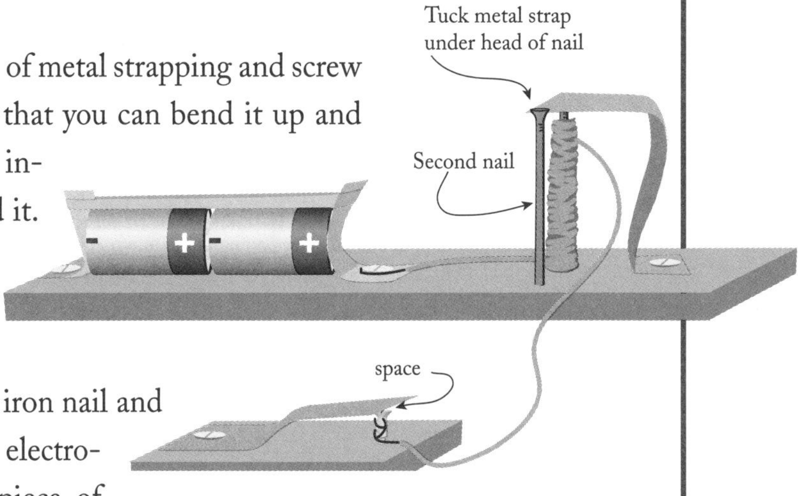

Now take the second iron nail and nail it in right next to the metal strapping, close to the nail with the wire wrapped around it, so the metal strapping is tucked just under the head of the nail. This nail will keep the metal strapping from pulling too far from the electromagnet. It also makes a clicking sound when the metal strapping is released by the magnet and moves upward.

Finally, take a small piece of the wire and attach it to the other screw holding down the key. Take the other end of this wire and attach it to the screw holding the other side of the battery holder onto the wood.

How to operate the telegraph:

When you push down on the telegraph key so it touches the screw, you complete the circuit, and allow electricity to flow from the batteries through the sounder's coil. As the metal strip hits the nail in the center of the coil it makes a clicking sound. When you release the key, it breaks the circuit and the metal strip hits the other nail, making a different clicking noise, and these two sounds form the dots and dashes of Morse code.

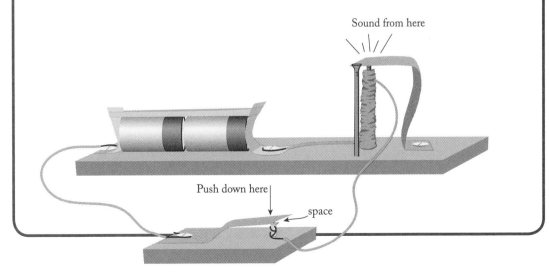

SIGNAL FLAGS

In addition to communicating by telegraph, both armies in the Civil War communicated by signal flags in a system known as wig-wag. The signal system was developed in the 1850s by an Army doctor named Albert Myer, who created it based on his doctoral dissertation on sign language for deaf people.

The system was designed so soldiers could communicate visual signals to each other over long distances—up to a few miles away. Depending on where they were and the weather conditions, soldiers used one of three flags: a white flag with a red square on it, a red flag with a white square on it, or a black flag with a white square on it. If the soldier was signaling from a hill or at sea, a red flag would be more easily seen; if he was signaling from a wooded area, a white flag would show up better, and if it was snowy, a black flag would be most visible. At night, signalmen replaced their flags with torches, always keeping another one at their feet as backup.

Signaling in wig-wag could be very dangerous work: the signalmen had to be fairly high up so that the signals could be seen from a distance, and if his fellow soldiers could see the signalman, so could the enemy. Usually the signal station would be at the highest point

Signal station on the Ogeechee River at Fort McAllister. Savannah, Georgia, vicinity.

closest to, but not directly in, the battle area. Sometimes, though, there were no hills or naturally high places, so troops would build towers for signal stations. These made members of the signal corps especially visible targets for the enemy.

THE WIG-WAG CODE

Each letter of the wig-wag alphabet was represented by a certain position or movement of the flag. In wig-wag code, messages were spelled out according to a letter–number code. Each letter of the alphabet was represented by a combination of numbers, and the numbers corresponded to flag movement. A

Signal Corps, Central Signal Station, Washington, D.C.

movement to the left of the center meant a "1," and a movement to the right of center meant a "2." The letter A, for example, was "11," which is two movements from the left to the center in a row. Dipping the flag forward one or more times signaled the end of a word, sentence, or message.

Both Confederate and Union signal corps units became very skilled at sending messages via wig-wag. Of course, since the system was visual, both sides could also "read" each other's messages, so each side developed wig-wag codes so the other side couldn't understand the messages being relayed. One way signalers tried to confuse their enemies was to use a pre-assigned letter for certain common or pre-arranged phrases—kind of a secret shorthand—followed by the signal for the number three to show that the single letter or double letter stood alone. For example, the letter "A" could be agreed-upon code for "artillery," so the signalman would signal, "1 1 3." The enemy would know it was the letter "A," but not what the A stood for. Both the

SIGNAL FLAG STARS

While most signal flags had a square in the middle, some Signal Corps officers were awarded a signal flag with a red star in the center. These were special flags given to officers who had done a great job in combat. The points of the star sometimes had the names of specific battles written on them where the Signal Corp unit had been especially effective in battle.

Union and Confederate Signal Corps spent lots of time and energy inventing new codes and trying to break each other's codes.

The Confederates first used the wig-wag signaling system in combat during the Battle of First Manassas (known to the Union as the First Battle of Bull Run). A signalman who was standing on a hilltop saw the shine of bayonets and signaled to his fellow soldiers, "Look out for your left; you are turned." His signal helped the Confederates win the battle.

CIVIL WAR FACTS & TRIVIA

★ *In the Union army, only officers were trusted with the signal code. They would call out the number combinations to Signal Corp sergeants, who would actually move the flag. Many sergeants learned the code through continued use. The Confederates, on the other hand, taught all of their Signal Corps personnel the code.*

★ *Signal flag stations were used primarily for two purposes: as message centers, and as lookout posts.*

★ *Signal flags were used in three different sizes: the smallest signal flags were 2 feet by 2 feet square, with an 8-inch center square. The next size flags were 4 by 4 feet, with a 16-inch square in the middle, and the largest signal flags were 6 feet square with a 2-foot square in the center.*

Signal tower overlooking Antietam Battlefield, Elk Mountain, Maryland.

LET'S GET STARTED

MAKE YOUR OWN SIGNAL FLAG

WHAT YOU'LL NEED

★ **old pillowcase** (white preferred, but any very light color will do)

★ **scissors**

★ **red paint, red duct or electrical tape, or red felt**

★ **wooden dowel rod,** five feet long

WHAT TO DO

1. Cut the pillow case so you have equal sides (you can use the other side to make another signal flag).

2. Sketch a square in the center of the flag.

3. Color the square with red paint or cover it with red duct or electrical tape.

Learn Wig-Wag Signals

In wig-wag code, messages are spelled out according to a letter-number code. Each letter of the alphabet is represented by a combination of numbers, and the numbers correspond to flag movement. A movement to the left of the center means a "1," and a movement to the right of center means a "2." The letter A, for example, is "11," which is two movements from the left to the center in a row. Dipping the flag forward one or more times signals the end of a word, sentence, or message.

troops in standardized uniforms so that they could tell themselves apart from the enemy. Some Southern militias had blue uniforms that looked almost identical to the Union army's blue jackets, and some Northern militia units had uniforms that looked nothing like standard Union clothes. So shortly after the war began, both armies set out rules for what its soldiers would wear.

The Union army's standard uniform was a blue wool suit made from material called "shoddy," with a long jacket (unless you were in the cavalry and then your jacket was shorter). At the beginning of the war, the uniform pants were dark blue, but later in the war the regulation uniform was a dark blue coat with light blue pants. Each soldier also had a belt set that had a cartridge box, a bayo-net and scabbard for his rifle, a canteen and canvas backpack, and a blanket roll with a half-shelter, wool blanket, and sometimes a rubber blanket or poncho. Union soldiers kept their socks, tooth-brush, writing implements, razors, and other personal items stowed inside their blanket rolls.

The Southern army's official uni-form was a short jacket and pants made of something called "jean," which was a rugged blend of cotton and wool, dyed

KNOW YOUR SLANG
....
housewife—sewing kit
....
chicken guts—officer's gold braiding on his cuff
....
duds—clothing
....
Zuzu—Zouaves

1—Highlanders, 79th Reg.
2—2nd Battalion, B. L. I.
3—Duryea's Zouaves, 5th N. Y. Reg.
4—Ellsworth Zouaves, 1st Reg. N. Y.
5—Seventh Reg. N. Y. S. M.
6—Salem Zouaves, Co. A, 8th Reg.
7—Sixth Mass. Reg.
8—Fourth Battalion, N. E. G.
9—Cobb's Light Battery.
10—National Lancers, 1st Bat. M. S. M.

Pictorial envelope depicting different regimental uniforms.

COLORS FOR DIFFERENT BRANCHES
One of the ways to tell different divisions apart on the battlefield was by the color of the trim on their uniforms. Different army divisions wore different colored trim, and both Union and Confederate soldiers used the same color coding. Cavalrymen wore yellow trim on their uniforms, dragoons wore orange, mounted rifleman wore emerald green, infantry wore light or "French," blue, and artillerymen wore red. Medical personnel wore black trim on their uniforms, and generals, staff, and engineer officers wore buff (cream) colored trim. Officers wore a stripe sewn down the leg of their pants, and the stripe would be in the color of their division.

ZOUAVE UNIFORMS

The most popular non-standard uniforms worn by both Northern and Southern soldiers were known as Zouave uniforms. They consisted of baggy, colorful pants that bloused at the ankle, white gaiters worn over their shoes, a wide sash, a short jacket worn over a plain shirt, and a white turban or fez.

gray or brown. Southern soldiers almost never had as much gear as Northern soldiers, mostly because there were so many shortages in the South that the supplies just weren't available.

The Union army had an easier time outfitting its troops, since most of the garment factories were in the North and they could get good-quality material from Europe. However, the army still had a difficult time getting uniforms to its soldiers because of the amount of time it took to make them. All clothing up to the 1860s was custom-made, and a single uniform could take as much as 14 hours to finish. The Union army solved some of its uniform problems by creating mass-produced clothing in just a few sizes: small, medium, and large. They figured that most soldiers would fit pretty well into one of the standard sizes,

Officers of Third Pennsylvania Heavy Artillery in their uniforms, Fort Monroe, Virginia.

and the rest would have to make do. This is the first time lots of clothing was made to fit a lot of people pretty well, rather than making a little bit of clothing fit one person perfectly, and it became the standard way of manufacturing clothing all over the world after the war.

CIVIL WAR FACTS & TRIVIA

★ *Union soldiers nicknamed Confederates "butternuts" because the dye used to make the Southern uniforms, which was derived from actual butternuts, was often uneven and turned a tan-gray color over time.*

KNOW YOUR SLANG
....
Graybacks—Southern soldiers
....
fresh fish—new recruits

★ *The wool blend material known as "shoddy" that was used to make the Union uniforms was of such poor quality and fell apart so quickly that the word "shoddy" quickly came to mean "of poor quality" or "poorly made."*

ZOUAVE

Zouave comes from an Algerian word, and the original Zouave units were native Algerian and North African fighters who joined the French Foreign Legion. They were known for their fierce fighting style, flashy uniforms, and incredible bravery. Interest in the Zouave fighters was sparked in the United States primarily because of a man named Elmer Ephraim Ellsworth. He learned about Zouave fighters while in Europe, and decided to start his own militia unit devoted to Zouave-style drilling. His Zouave unit toured the country, amazing audiences with their drilling skill and fancy uniforms and sparking a "Zouave fever" in the 1850s. When the war broke out, Zouave units fought in both Confederate and Union armies, although some soldiers changed to traditional uniforms when they realized that their colorful clothes made them a more visible target.

Band of the One hundred and fourteenth Pennsylvania Infantry (Zouaves), Brandy Station, Virginia.

MAKE YOUR OWN UNION OR CONFEDERATE JACKET

WHAT YOU'LL NEED

★ **old suit jacket:** man's blue jacket for a Union uniform, or a woman's (shorter) gray or light brown jacket for a Confederate uniform (check thrift stores or see if your parents have an old jacket).

★ **1 yard of felt** in light blue (infantry), red (artillery), green (mounted riflemen and sharpshooters), orange (dragoons), or yellow (regular cavalry)

★ **safety pins**

★ **needle and thread, fabric glue, or stapler**

★ **1 yard of braid or rickrack**

★ **brass buttons** (optional)

WHAT TO DO

1. Take the collar of the suit jacket and pull it up so it stands up. Fold the lapels inside the jacket so that only the collar is out. This is the style of jacket that soldiers wore back then. You can either trim the lapels to make them fit more easily inside the jacket, or press them with an iron. Then safety pin them to the inside so they don't fold back out.

fold lapels in, iron and pin in place

2. Decide what branch of the military you want to be. This will determine your felt color choice.

3. Make felt cuffs about four inches long to go over the wrists of your jacket, and make a felt collar cover. Safety pin, stitch, staple, or glue the cuffs and collar on to your jacket.

widest part of cuff to the outside of sleeve

staple or pin cuff together and pin to sleeve

4. Sew or glue your braid directly onto your coat. An officer would also have a stripe of braid on the outside of the pant leg to indicate a higher rank. If you really want to get crazy and be a general or other very high-ranking officer, you can sew two rows of buttons down the front of your suit. The double row of buttons indicated high rank and could be seen from a distance.

LET'S GET STARTED

MAKE YOUR OWN FORAGE CAP

The forage cap or kepi was the standard issue cap for all enlisted men in the Union army and most of the Confederate army, as well.

WHAT YOU'LL NEED

* **tape measure**
* **scissors**
* **black or gray felt,** sticky-backed if available
* **sheet of cardboard** or an old manila file folder
* **stapler**
* **glue stick**
* **gold or black pipe cleaner or ribbon**

WHAT TO DO

1. Use the tape measure to take a rough measurement of your head. Felt usually comes in 8½-by-11-inch sheets, and most kids can make a hat that will fit simply by cutting one sheet of felt lengthwise, down the middle. This will give you two 4¼-

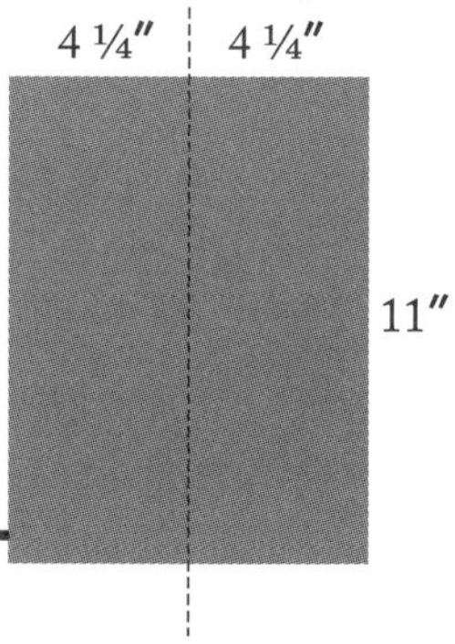

4 ¼″   4 ¼″

11″

by-11-inch pieces of felt. If your head is bigger than this, cut another piece of felt down the middle. You can use one of these extra strips to make the hat larger if you need it.

2. Cut four strips of cardboard approximately 8 inches long by 2 inches wide. These will form the base of your hat.

3. Staple three of the four cardboard strips together lengthwise. Wrap this strip around your head. If it is too small, add another cardboard strip and measure again. Staple the ends together so that the cardboard ring fits snugly on your head, then cut off any extra cardboard.

4. Take one of the felt strips and staple it to the cardboard ring: the bottom of the long end of the felt should line up with the bottom edge of the cardboard ring so that the cardboard ring is completely covered. Then take the second strip and do the same. Tuck any extra felt from the second strip under the first so that when you're done, you'll have a complete circle of felt.

felt

cardboard

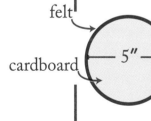

5"

5. The top of the kepi is smaller than the headband. Make a circle out of cardboard that's about 5 inches in diameter (see the template on page 132). Make a circle of felt about half an inch wider than the cardboard circle, and glue the two circles together.

6. Now lay the circle over the top edge of the hat. Since the top of the hat is smaller than the bottom make the felt overlap at the top, so it fits the circle (see diagram). Staple or glue the top sides of the hat to keep this shape.

glue

fold over,
glue down edges

7. Put glue around the outside rim of the circle and lay the hat on the circle. Pull the ends of the circle around the hat so the glue has something to adhere to. If you're using sticky felt, you shouldn't have any problem making the circle stick to the sides of the hat felt.

8. Now you need to make the bill. Trace template B from page 134 onto a piece of cardboard. Glue a matching piece of felt to one side. Trace template C from page 134 onto another piece of felt and glue that to the other side of the cardboard. This will be the bottom of your hat bill, and will attach the bill to the cardboard rim inside the hat.

B   B   C

glue felt B onto
cardboard B

glue felt C onto
other side of
cardboard B

9. Glue the felt rim of the bill onto the cardboard rim inside the hat. Let sit until it's dry. If you are having trouble keeping it on with glue, staple it on—the staples will be covered by the trim ribbon.

10. Finally, cut a piece of ribbon or pipe cleaner long enough to go around the front of your hat. If you're making a Confederate hat, use black. If you're making a Union hat, use gold. Glue the ribbon to the seam on the hat, just above the bill.

glue

attach glued tab to
inside front of cap

MAKE YOUR OWN ZOUAVE FEZ

Unlike kepis, fezzes are stiff hats that perch on top of the head rather than slouch down.

WHAT YOU'LL NEED

- ★ **red or black felt**
- ★ **sheet of cardboard** or old manila file folder
- ★ **glue stick**
- ★ **scissors**
- ★ **yarn** for tassel

WHAT TO DO

1. Follow step one from the forage cap project for measuring your head and cutting felt.

2. Cut four strips of cardboard, each approximately 4 inches long by 5 inches wide.

3. Staple three of the four cardboard strips together lengthwise. Wrap this strip around your head snugly, so that the cardboard strips make a kind of cone shape. If it is too small, add another cardboard strip and measure again.

4. Glue the felt to the outside of the cardboard, covering it completely. Then refit the hat to your head and staple the ends together so that the cardboard ring fits snugly on your head.

5. The top of the fez is smaller than the headband. Make a circle out of cardboard that's about 4 inches in diameter. Cut a circle of felt about half an inch wider than the cardboard circle, and glue the two circles together. See the template on page 129.

4″

hole

glue

tie knot

6. Poke a small hole in the center of the circle, and thread a tassel through the hole. Tie a knot in the end of the yarn on the inside, so when the top of the hat is glued to the sides, the tassel will be on the outside.

7. Now turn the hat over and fit the circle on to the top edge of the felt. Then put glue around the outside rim of the circle and lay the hat on the circle. Pull the ends of the circle around the hat so the glue has something to adhere to. If you're using sticky felt, you shouldn't have any problem making the circle stick to the sides of the hat felt.

KNOW YOUR SLANG

hayfoot, strawfoot—command used to teach new soldiers the difference between left (hayfoot) and right (strawfoot)

Bummer's cap—regulation fatigue or forage cap

Bummer—a loafer, a forager, or someone safe in the rear

MAKE LIKE A ZOUAVE

Most Civil War soldiers who wore fezzes were part of Zouave units and wore the Zouave uniform. You can make a modified Zouave uniform by wearing baggy sweatpants stuffed into white sports socks, a solid color long-sleeve T-shirt, and a vest. You may feel like a clown, but many modern clown costumes—such as some Shriners wear—bear a striking similarity to the Zouave uniforms that militia units wore during the Civil War.

ON THE HOMEFRONT

No one in either the North or South thought the war would run more than a few months, or that it would cause the destruction, turmoil, or loss of life that it did over the course of four bloody years.

Many civilians in the North were affected by the war primarily through shortages of certain goods, and the absence of fathers, sons, and husbands to help run farms, businesses, and households. In contrast, daily life for people in the South could be a terrible struggle. The vast majority of battles were fought in the Southern states, and thousands of troops moved through large areas of the South—troops that needed food, shelter, and supplies that were provided at the expense of Southern civilians. As the war years went by, more and more of the South was retaken by the Union, and the Union policy of "total war" (completely destroying an enemy's means of fighting a war) meant that many parts of the South were completely ravaged: crops ruined, livestock slaughtered, and fields made untillable.

Burned out section of Richmond, Virginia.

Federal pickets outside the city of Atlanta, Georgia.

The biggest problem for people in the South was the shortage of food. This was a huge problem in many Southern cities, especially those that the Union considered strategic. Union troops would blockade these cities, not allowing supplies of any kind, including food, to reach the citizens. The people of Richmond, Virginia, for example, suffered from such severe food shortages that in the spring of 1863, women began rioting in what became known as the Richmond Bread Riots—and this was a full two years before the official end of the war. Another part of the problem was that most of the land in the South had been traditionally devoted to growing cotton, not food crops.

Surprisingly, another major shortage in the Confederate states was fabric—although the Southern states produced the majority of the cotton used to make cloth, the Union states had most of the industry, including textile mills. While Northern women experienced

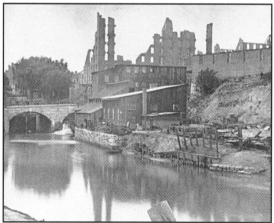

James River and Kanawha Canal near the Haxall Flour Mills in Richmond, Virginia.

Ruins of a Southern paper mill with water wheel.

some temporary fabric shortages because of the loss of Southern cotton, Southern women used up every kind of fabric they could, both to help the war effort, and to clothe themselves and their families. Many Southern women learned how to sew, knit, and spin—often for the first time, since wealthy families had always relied on slaves to do this kind of work. "Homespun" dresses—dresses made from cotton spun and sewed by hand—became very common.

In both the North and the South, many women discovered that the war allowed them to have roles outside their traditional ones as mothers, daughters, and wives. Women became active in supporting the war effort in many different ways: participating in Ladies' Aid Societies, nursing, even acting as spies, and, in a very few cases, disguising themselves as men and becoming soldiers. Many women took over traditionally male roles in their households, including overseeing plantations and farms and running businesses. What's more, many discovered that they both liked the responsibility and were very good at it.

Despite the overwhelming hardships of life in wartime, people still had fun, held parties and dances, and lived their day-to-day lives as best they could. Minstrel shows were a popular form of live entertainment during the Civil War, as were live band concerts and traveling circuses. Children played with dolls and wooden toys, and played a new game that was becoming incredibly popular throughout the North and South: baseball.

When the war officially ended in 1865, life in the re-United States was forever changed. Slaves who had never known independence were able to start their lives anew as free people. Southerners had to rebuild their homes, lives, and land, without the benefit of slave labor. Northerners had to readjust to a postwar economy and the influx of thousands of men who were returning to a workforce that wasn't ready for them. In addition, families had to adjust to being together again with men who had lived through experiences that were hard to bear and even harder to forget.

BERRY INK AND HOMEMADE PAPER

Resources of all kinds—food, fuel, clothing, and shoes—were in short supply as the Civil War dragged on, especially in the South. Everyone in the Confederate states experienced shortages, but the hardest hit were the Southern poor. Life was never very easy for many people in the South, but hard times were made much harder by shortages of food, farming help, and basic household items that were previously manufactured in the North and shipped south. Everyday living became challenging for many Southerners, and even simple things like writing a letter took some ingenuity.

The main form of communication between families and soldiers was through letter writing, and it was also a way for many soldiers to pass long hours at camp. Most soldiers begged their families to write back to them right away, and receiving a letter from home was the highlight of most soldiers' day.

Soldiers had to buy their own paper and pens to write letters, and they also had to buy stamps. Later in the war, organizations such as the U.S. Christian Commission and U.S. Sanitary Commission gave out paper and envelopes to soldiers free of charge. In 1864, the U.S. Mail Service announced that Union

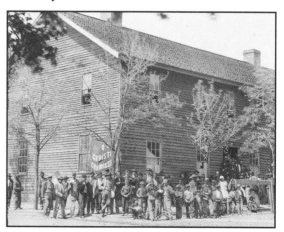

Crowd outside the headquarters of the U.S. Christian Commission. Richmond, Virginia.

soldiers could send their letters home for free as long as they wrote "soldier's letter" on the outside of the envelope. The Confederates, on the other hand, didn't have that option, and shortages in paper, stamps, and even writing implements became much worse as the war dragged on.

People did not let the chronic shortages of supplies such as ink or writing paper keep them from corresponding with their friends and relatives, how-

> ## CONFEDERATE MAIL ROUTES
>
> *When the Civil War began, the Confederates created their own postal system and mail routes. Most of the mail during that time was coordinated through Vicksburg, Mississippi, and was transported via steamboats. Mail was also carried over land by stagecoach or a single rider on a horse.*
>
> **VICKSBURG, MISSISSIPPI**

ever. If they were determined to write a letter, they found resources to help them complete their task. They created ink from the juice of berries. When they ran out of stationery, they used any scraps of paper they could find, from old newspapers to political billets.

CIVIL WAR FACTS & TRIVIA

★ *Soldiers would write letters home to their families in between battles. Because mail delivery did not take place on a regular basis, sometimes they would end up sending home six or more letters at one time. They would number each letter so their families could read them in the order they were written.*

★ *No Confederate postage stamps were available after the Confederate Post Office Department assumed operation of the postal system on June 1, 1861, so postmasters had to use hand stamps or manuscript markings to indicate postage paid (or due) during the Confederate stampless period. Single-rate postage was 5¢ for letters weighing less than half an ounce and sent distances less than 500 miles. Double-rate postage of 10¢ was charged for letters weighing more than a half ounce or sent distances more than 500 miles.*

★ *General McClellan took a portable printing press with him and printed troop bulletins when his regiment set up camp.*

★ LET'S GET STARTED ★

MAKE YOUR OWN BERRY INK

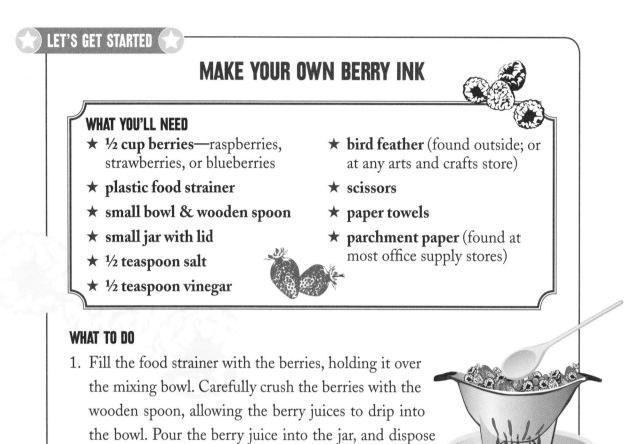

WHAT YOU'LL NEED

- ★ **½ cup berries**—raspberries, strawberries, or blueberries
- ★ **plastic food strainer**
- ★ **small bowl & wooden spoon**
- ★ **small jar with lid**
- ★ **½ teaspoon salt**
- ★ **½ teaspoon vinegar**
- ★ **bird feather** (found outside; or at any arts and crafts store)
- ★ **scissors**
- ★ **paper towels**
- ★ **parchment paper** (found at most office supply stores)

WHAT TO DO

1. Fill the food strainer with the berries, holding it over the mixing bowl. Carefully crush the berries with the wooden spoon, allowing the berry juices to drip into the bowl. Pour the berry juice into the jar, and dispose of the berry pulp that is left in the strainer.

2. Add the salt and the vinegar to the berry juice and stir until the salt has dissolved. If the berry ink seems to be too thick, add a small amount of water. Be careful, however, as adding water may dilute the bright color of the juice.

3. Carefully cut the end of the feather at a curved angle, creating a fairly sharp point. You may also want to clean out the end of the quill.

4. Use the parchment paper to practice writing, blotting the extra ink with the paper towel. Start with lines and curves, and when you get the hang of using the quill, start writing. Experiment with different ways and angles of holding the quill and different amounts of ink.

MAKE YOUR OWN HANDMADE PAPER

Here's a great way to make your own writing paper using recycled material

WHAT YOU'LL NEED

★ **scrap paper** torn into 1-by-1-inch pieces (paper towels, construction paper, and tissue paper work well). The amount you'll need will vary, but at least four or five pieces' worth

★ **2 large tubs or pots** One is for soaking the torn paper; the other is for making paper and needs to be larger than the frame you use to make the paper (the frame will need to lay flat in the pot).

★ **wire clothes hanger** for frame
★ **old nylon stocking**
★ **stapler**
★ **blender**
★ **sponge**
★ **dishtowels, felt, or newsprint** for blotting

★ **rolling pin**
★ **household iron**
★ **strainer**
★ **pieces of colored construction paper, colored thread,** or **dried flowers or herbs** (optional)

WHAT TO DO

1. Soak the torn paper pieces in warm water for at least 30 minutes. If possible, leave it soaking overnight.

2. Bend the wire hanger to make a square-shaped frame. Cover your hanger with a nylon stocking and staple it in place to make a screen.

3. Fill the blender halfway with warm water, then add a handful of the soaked paper. Making sure the lid is on tight, blend at medium speed until you no longer see pieces of paper (the pulp has a soupy consistency called a slurry).

You can blend in a piece of construction paper for color, or stir in short pieces of thread, dried flowers, or herbs for texture.

4. Pour the blended mixture into the large tub and then fill the tub with warm water to cover the mixture, stirring thoroughly until the ingredients are evenly dispersed.

5. Slide your frame into the tub, allowing some pulp to settle onto the screen. Hold the frame underwater, and gently move it back and forth to get an even layer of fibers on the screen.

6. Lift the frame out of the mixture, keeping it flat. Allow it to drip over the tub until most of the water has drained through. You should have a uniform layer of the pulp mixture on the screen. Press the pulp gently with your hand to squeeze out excess moisture. Soak up excess water from the bottom of the screen with a sponge.

7. Place clean dishtowels, felt, or newspaper on a flat surface and flip the screen paper-side-down onto the cloth. Lift the screen gently, leaving behind the paper. This is called couching.

8. Cover the paper with another cloth or piece of felt, and squeeze out moisture using a rolling pin. Make as many sheets as you like, and place the sheets out of the way to dry. You may want to let the paper dry overnight.

9. When the paper is mostly dry, you may use an iron at a medium heat setting to fully dry it. When the paper is dry, pull the cloth gently from both ends, stretching it to loosen the paper from the cloth. Gently peel off the paper.

10. When you're finished making paper, collect the leftover pulp in a strainer and throw it out, or freeze it in a plastic bag for future use. Don't pour the pulp down the drain—it will clog your pipes.

CIVIL WAR QUILTS

Although most women weren't fighting on the battlefield during the Civil War, women played a hugely important role supporting the troops and keeping things together back home.

As the men left home to fight, women struggled to keep farms going and businesses surviving, and to feed and clothe their families. It was often very difficult, especially for women on small farms who relied on everyone in the family for help.

When times were particularly tough and food especially scarce, communities in the South would sometimes create fundraising quilts. Made of donated cloth scraps and pieced together by a church group or at a community quilting bee, they were then sold at church bazaars to raise money for families who were especially hard hit.

In the North, abolitionists would hold Abolitionist Fairs, similar to crafts fairs, where women who supported the anti-slavery cause would donate quilts and other

Mary Tippee, sutler with Collis Zouaves,
One hundred and fourteenth Pennsylvania.

THE BONNET BRIGADES

When war broke out in 1861, the first Ladies' Aid societies sprang up all over the Northern states. Women organized themselves into what were sometimes called bonnet brigades, to provide soldiers going to battle with whatever supplies they might need, from bandages and food to clothes. The Ladies' Aid societies were well-organized and full of well-meaning and enthusiastic volunteers, but because they were run by individual groups of women throughout the North, their efforts weren't very well coordinated. Some troops would get far too many supplies, while others didn't get any. Sometimes the supplies would be spoiled before they reached the soldiers, and sometimes the quality of what the women made was so bad they were unusable. In order to better regulate the quality and quantity of supplies reaching the troops, in 1862 the U.S. Sanitary Commission was formed to distribute all the supplies to the Union army and inspect camps and hospitals for the North. Many women volunteered to be part of the U.S. Sanitary Commission, and the Ladies' Aid societies eventually died out.

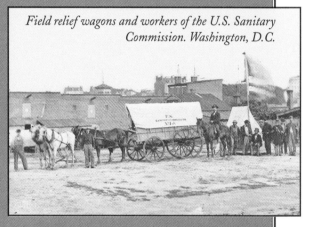

Field relief wagons and workers of the U.S. Sanitary Commission. Washington, D.C.

needlework to be sold to raise money for the abolitionists. Often these quilts would have anti-slavery poems and sayings embroidered on them.

One of the most common quilt patterns during the Civil War was called Jacob's Ladder, or simply Four Patch; it was a traditional quilt pattern made up of small squares sewn together to look like the steps of a ladder. This pattern later became known as the Underground Railroad, because of stories told after the war about how the quilts directed runaway slaves to the path of freedom via the Underground Railroad.

Another quilt pattern, the Log Cabin (later known as Lincoln's Log Cabin), was also rumored to provide information to slaves traveling to freedom: stories say that

SOUTHERN GUNBOAT QUILTS

The South had its own groups of Ladies' Aid societies, made up of volunteers who banded together to support their husbands, sons, and brothers on the battlefield. At the beginning of the war, one of the things the Confederates lacked most was gunboats, and Southern Ladies' Aid societies enthusiastically supported the Confederate cause by making gunboat quilts that they sold or raffled off to raise money. By the end of 1862, enough money had been raised to buy three gunboats, but by this time the Confederate navy had suffered so many defeats that it was likely that their seaports would fall to the Union. Ladies' Aid societies then turned their skills to supporting the troops, and they spent much of their energy creating clothing and bedding.

if a quilt hung in a house window or on a clothesline had a Log Cabin design with a black center square (red center squares were more common), it meant that the house was an Underground Railroad stop.

Unfortunately, historians have never found first-hand evidence of slaves or people who worked in the Underground Railroad mentioning these coded quilts. In fact, the first quilt with a Log Cabin pattern wasn't made in the United States until the Civil War was almost over, and by that time the Underground Railroad wasn't active in the same way it had been before the war began.

CIVIL WAR FACTS & TRIVIA

★ *Quilts made for soldiers during the Civil War often had inspiring words embroidered on them to encourage the soldiers on the battlefield. Many times soldiers would write to the women who made them, thanking them for their quilts. This would sometimes lead to letter-writing exchanges between soldiers and single women, and at least a few soldiers married the women who made quilts for them.*

★ *Female anti-slavery societies were founded by white and free black women in the Northern states many years before the Civil War. They raised money to publicize their cause, opened schools for black children, and circulated petitions to raise awareness about the evils of slavery.*

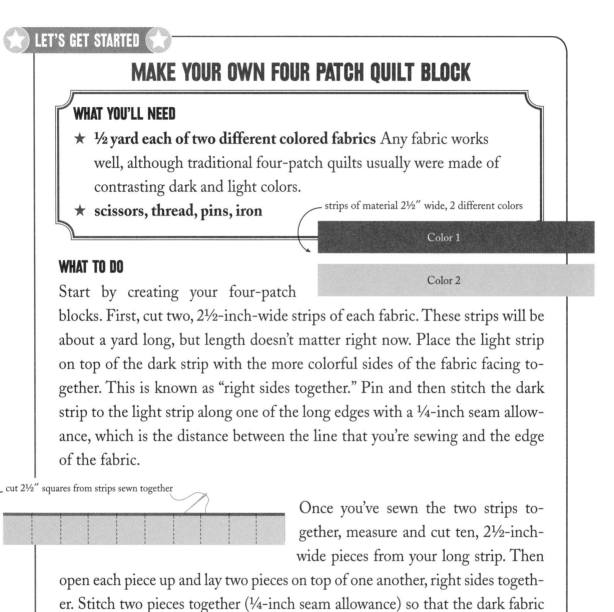

★ **LET'S GET STARTED** ★

MAKE YOUR OWN FOUR PATCH QUILT BLOCK

WHAT YOU'LL NEED

★ **½ yard each of two different colored fabrics** Any fabric works well, although traditional four-patch quilts usually were made of contrasting dark and light colors.

★ **scissors, thread, pins, iron**

strips of material 2½″ wide, 2 different colors

Color 1

Color 2

WHAT TO DO

Start by creating your four-patch blocks. First, cut two, 2½-inch-wide strips of each fabric. These strips will be about a yard long, but length doesn't matter right now. Place the light strip on top of the dark strip with the more colorful sides of the fabric facing together. This is known as "right sides together." Pin and then stitch the dark strip to the light strip along one of the long edges with a ¼-inch seam allowance, which is the distance between the line that you're sewing and the edge of the fabric.

cut 2½″ squares from strips sewn together

Once you've sewn the two strips together, measure and cut ten, 2½-inch-wide pieces from your long strip. Then open each piece up and lay two pieces on top of one another, right sides together. Stitch two pieces together (¼-inch seam allowance) so that the dark fabric and light fabric are opposite each other, like a checkerboard. Make five of these four-patch blocks. They will be approximately 4¼ inches square.

cut 4 squares of each color - 4⅞″

Now you'll create setting triangles, which make the four-patch squares stand out and will result in a diagonal pattern on your quilt block.

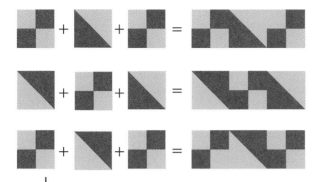

To create setting triangles, cut two, 4⅞-inch squares of each color fabric (dark and light—see the template on page 133). Cut each square in half diagonally and sew one dark triangle to one light triangle (with a ¼-inch seam allowance) to make a square. When you're done you'll have four, 4¼-inch squares made up of dark and light triangles.

If you iron all of your blocks they will lie flat and the next stage will be easier. Line up your four-patch blocks and your setting triangle blocks in the pattern shown above. Put the middle patch of the first row on top of the first patch in that row, with right sides together. Pin and sew down the right side. Open up the fabric, and place the third patch in the first row on top of the second patch in that row, right sides together, and sew down the right side. Do the same for the other two rows you've laid out in a pattern. When you're done you'll have three strips of three squares sewn together.

Now take the top strip and place it on the middle strip, right sides together. Pin the strips in place along the top edge. (Open it up to check that you have the correct edges pinned before you stitch.) Sew one long seam across the entire length of the two strips. Open up the fabric, and place the bottom strip of squares on the middle strip, right sides together. Pin the strips together along the bottom edge (open it up to check), and sew one long seam across the entire length of these two strips.

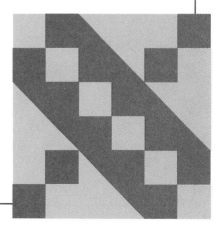

Open up the fabric, and you will have a nine-patch quilt square! Use the iron again to press your square for a nice, finished look.

MAKE YOUR OWN PILLOW OR WALL HANGING

You can easily make your four patch quilt square into a finished pillow or wall hanging.

WHAT YOU'LL NEED

★ finished quilt square

★ ½ yard of fabric

★ scissors

★ pins, needle, thread

★ iron

★ pillow stuffing

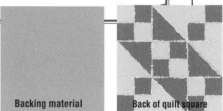

Backing material

Back of quilt square

WHAT TO DO

1. Cut a square out of the fabric measuring 11¾ inches by 11¾ inches. Lay it on a work surface with the right side up. Lay your quilt square on top of the fabric square with the right side down (so right sides are together). Pin completely around three of the sides, and one quarter of the way from each corner on the fourth side. If any of the edges don't line up well you can trim a bit to make them even. Stitch these seams together leaving a ¼-inch seam allowance.

Back of quilt square on top of backing piece

pin quilt square to backing piece

2. Turn the pillowcase right side out so that the seams are on the inside. Press with the iron, pushing the seam allowance at the open gap to the inside. If you are making a wall hanging, stitch the gap closed. For a pillow, stuff the case with pillow stuffing and then sew the gap closed.

sew quilt square to backing piece leaving gap on 1 side

turn right side out

MAKE YOUR OWN FOUR PATCH QUILT

If you want to continue and make an entire quilt, simply make more big squares. You can then sew all of the big squares together into a quilt.

WHAT YOU'LL NEED

★ **cotton or synthetic batting** the same size or slightly larger than your quilt top

★ **backing material** of any color or pattern approximately the same thickness as your top layer, the same size or slightly larger than your quilt top

★ **needle, thread, and scissors**

★ **yarn or embroidery floss**

★ **iron**

★ **binding tape** for the outside edges

quilt squares
batting
backing material-right side DOWN

WHAT TO DO

1. Piece the big squares together according to the diagram. Iron the quilt top so it lays flat. Place the backing right-side-down on the floor, with the batting on top of it and the quilt top right-side-up on top of that, so that you have the three layers in the correct order.

2. Sew around the outside of your quilt, sewing the three layers together. Cut off any excess batting and backing material.

quilt squares
batting
backing material-right side DOWN

3. Thread a piece of yarn or embroidery floss through a needle, and make a stitch through the three layers of backing, batting, and quilt top at each corner of each four-patch block, and tie a bow at the top to hold the stitch in place. This will keep the batting from shifting inside your quilt.

4. Finish the edges. A very easy way to finish the edges of your quilt is to use binding tape. It comes in many colors and you can buy it at any fabric store. Measure the sides of your quilt and cut the binding tape to fit. Sew the binding tape on all sides, tucking one piece of tape under another at the corners.

You'll have a beautiful Civil War quilt!

CIVIL WAR DOLLS

During the Civil War era, most American children played with dolls that were simple and homemade. By the mid-1800s dollmakers in Europe were famous for creating wooden, porcelain, and even wax dolls with very lifelike features, and these dolls were certainly available to some American children—probably more to look at than to play with. Most children, though, played with dolls that were made by family members using supplies that were close at hand. Depending on where in the country they lived, this meant that their dolls were usually made of wood, rags, or corn husks.

Probably the most common doll made for little girls during the mid-1800s was the rag doll. These were popular in both the North and the South, and there were many different ways to make them. In the South, rag dolls were often called hankie dolls or plantation dolls (and sometimes also called church dolls, since they were made of soft cotton and wouldn't make a lot of noise if they fell on the floor during church). Rag dolls were made out of

Rag doll that was in the room where Robert E. Lee surrendered to Ulysses S. Grant.

THE "SILENT WITNESS" DOLL

One particular rag doll played a famous role in the surrender of General Robert E. Lee to General Ulysses S. Grant at Appomattox Court House on April 9, 1865. The two generals met in a house owned by a man named Wilmer McLean. He had a daughter named Lula who was playing with a rag doll in the room where the two gener–als were to meet and sign the conditions of surrender. When Lula saw soldiers come into the house, she ran outside, leaving the doll be–hind. The doll was the "silent witness" to the surrender, and when Lee left to tell his troops of the surrender, a Union soldier (Lieutenant Colonel Thomas W.C. Moore) picked up the rag doll and took it with him.

McLean house.
Appomattox Court House, Virginia.

a soft piece of cotton fabric with cotton stuffing for its head. One variation of the rag doll was called a "sugar baby." Mothers would make a rag doll and put sugar cubes in the head portion for their young kids to suck on.

Another very common doll made by families in the Civil War was the corn husk doll. Corn was a crop grown in many parts of the country, and corn husks were plentiful. Depending on what color hair a girl wanted for her doll, she would take silk off the corn ears in the early, mid, or late season. Early-season corn held yellow silk, mid-season corn silk was reddish brown, and late-season silk was darker brown.

CIVIL WAR TRIVIA

★ *The first American patent for dollmaking was taken out a few years before the war, by a man named Ludwig Greiner. He made doll heads only—the bodies were made by people at home.*

MAKE YOUR OWN CORN HUSK DOLL

WHAT YOU'LL NEED

★ **corn husks** (It's better to start with green corn husks, but if you don't have any handy you can buy both green and dried husks in packages at local craft stores)

★ **large bowl** filled with warm water

★ **string**

★ **scissors**

WHAT TO DO

1. If you are using green husks, skip this step. If you are using dried husks, soak them in water until they are pliable. While the husks are soaking, cut a half dozen or so pieces of string, each about 5 inches in length.

2. Grab several large corn husks from the bowl and tie them together an inch or two down from one end. Pull the lengths of the husk down over what is to be the head part, like peeling a banana. Shape the head and tie string around what is to be the neck.

3. To make the doll's arms, remove three more husks from the bowl. Tie them together at one end, braid, and tie off. Cut the ends to make even. Place the arms between the lengths of husk then tie a piece of string around the doll's waist.

4. Crisscross thin strips of corn husk around the doll's chest, waist, and neck. Tuck the ends in (you can tie off the husk strips before tucking them in). Use thin husk strips to cover the strings at the doll's "wrists."

5. To fill out her skirt, trim the widest corn husks you have so they are approximately the same length. Wrap these husks around her middle and tie in place. Wrap her middle with a strip of husk, then trim the bottom of her skirt so it's even.

6. For hair, you can glue on dried corn silk, or take a large rectangular piece of husk, fold it, and tie it as a head scarf.

7. It's a good idea to let the doll dry, standing, on a flat surface.

CORN HUSKS can be soaked in food coloring to make colored clothing or skin. Soak husks for 30 minutes in a large bowl containing warm water and several drops of your desired color. To make vibrant browns, soak husks in a large bowl of coffee or tea.

⭐ **LET'S GET STARTED** ⭐

MAKE YOUR OWN RAG DOLL

WHAT YOU'LL NEED

★ **craft paper** or any other medium-weight paper

★ **pencils/pens**

★ **scissors**

★ **scrap fabric**

★ **pins, thread, needle**

★ **fabric paint, buttons, yarn** or whatever else you might want to decorate your doll

★ **filling**—polyester fiberfill works well, but you can use any other sort of soft filling fabric

Cut this line

Outline of doll

WHAT TO DO

1. To make a pattern for your doll, fold a piece of paper in half. Use a pencil to draw the outline of half of your doll onto the paper. This way the doll will be symmetrical. It should be a fairly simple design so it's easy to cut out. Add ½ inch around your doll's outline for a seam allowance. Cut the paper along the seam allowance and unfold the paper.

2. Place the pattern on your chosen fabric and pin it into place. Carefully cut around the pattern. Do this twice so that you have front and back sides for your doll.

3. Decorate your doll with paint if you want to, and allow it to dry before going on to the next step.

4. Pin the two sides together, with decorated sides FACING each other, and carefully sew together, ½ inch from the edge of the fabric. Leave a 2-to-3-inch section open where the dolls legs meet, and turn the doll right side out. Next, stuff the doll with filling and sew the gap closed.

Leave gap in seam to insert stuffing

5. Decorate more if you'd like with yarn for hair, buttons, markers, etc.

Insert stuffing in gap in seam

MAKE YOUR OWN HANKY DOLL

WHAT YOU'LL NEED

★ **one large handkerchief** of any color

★ **ribbon** (½-inch wide works best) or small rope or twine

★ **filling** such as cotton or fiberfill

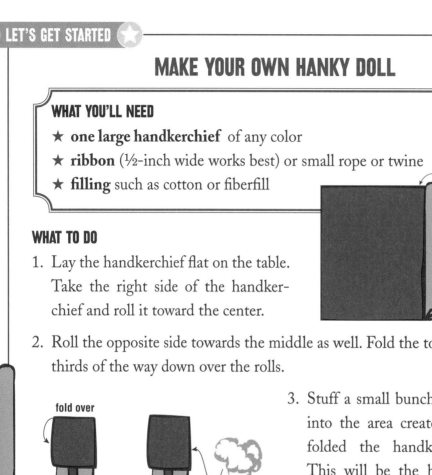

WHAT TO DO

1. Lay the handkerchief flat on the table. Take the right side of the handkerchief and roll it toward the center.

2. Roll the opposite side towards the middle as well. Fold the top about two-thirds of the way down over the rolls.

fold over

put stuffing in "pocket"

3. Stuff a small bunch of filling up into the area created when you folded the handkerchief over. This will be the head of the doll.

4. Tie a piece of ribbon or string where the neck of the doll should be, forming a head.

5. Reach into the rolls and pull out the corners, creating arms and hands. Do the same for the legs and feet. Your doll is now finished!

find corners and pull them out to form hands and feet

CIVILIAN FOOD

Before the start of the Civil War, most people in America had access to a variety of plentiful food. The food people ate in the 1850s and 1860s was different from what we eat today (no fast food, less variety), but a lot of the staple foods are similar. As soon as war broke out, however, food became scarce and expensive, especially for people in the South.

In the South, people suffered intensely because of food shortages. From the beginning of the war, the Union placed blockades on Confederate ports, disabling the South's ability to receive food via boat. The Union army was also relentless in attacking and pillaging Confederate towns, taking what resources they could find. Southern cities were especially hard hit by food shortages, although rural areas also felt the devastation, as battles fought in these areas would destroy crops and other food sources.

KNOW YOUR SLANG

long sweetening—molasses

goobers—peanuts

One way people preserved their food, especially fruits and vegetables, was to dry them. Dried fruits and vegetables could be safely stored in a cool, dry place

Harewood Hospital, on farm of W. W. Corcoran, Washington, D.C. Many farms were taken over for use by the military.

SOUTHERN FOOD PRICES

You think food is expensive today? Here is a list of how the price of food skyrocketed during the Civil War. To give you some perspective, a pound of gourmet coffee today is about $8.00, and a pound of butter is somewhere around $2.50.

1861: *bacon, 12.5 cents per pound; butter, 20 cents per pound; coffee, 35 cents per pound; flour, $6 per barrel*

1862: *bacon, 75 cents per pound; butter, 75 cents to $2 per pound; coffee, $1.50 to $4 per pound; flour, $16 to $40 per barrel*

1863: *bacon, $1.25 to $6 per pound; butter, $2 to $4 per pound; coffee, $5 to $30 per pound; flour, $30 to $75 per barrel*

1864: *bacon, $8 to $9 per pound; butter, $15 to $25 per pound; coffee, $12 to $60 per pound; flour, $125 to $500 per barrel*

1865: *bacon, $11 to $13 per pound; butter, $15 to $20 per pound; flour, $325 to $1000 per barrel*

for many months. Most farmers had root cellars where they kept barrels of dried fruits and vegetables, canned foods, and salted meats. The root cellars were usually simple rooms dug directly into the ground and covered by a door placed at ground level. The beauty of root cellars were that they stayed cool during the summer months, so food stored in them didn't spoil in hot and humid weather.

CIVIL WAR FACTS & TRIVIA

★ *Coffee was both the scarcest and most valued drink during the Civil War, and many people came up with interesting coffee substitutes, including okra seed, rice, wheat, peanuts, beans, sweet potatoes, peas, and acorns. These would be dried and then soaked in hot water, creating a coffee-like drink.*

★ *Since cane sugar and molasses were produced primarily in the South, prior to and during the war Northerners substituted maple sugar as an act of protest against the South.*

★ At the beginning of the Civil War, it is said that Northerners enjoyed tea, bread, scrambled eggs, fried fish, wild pigeon, and oysters for breakfast, while Southerners preferred fried chicken, bread with caviar, and mutton with onions for breakfast. As the war depleted resources, however, both groups were reduced to tea or coffee and bread for their morning meal—if that was even available.

★ During Sherman's march to the sea from August to November 1864, his troops burned and destroyed huundreds of barns full of grain, corn, and other crops that had just been harvested. Troops also killed barns full of livestock, leaving them dead in their pens. These Northern troops were called bummers because of this devastation, and the South's recovery was very slow and difficult as a result of the destruction of basic food supplies.

FUN AND SWEETS

Although time and supplies for parties were limited during the Civil War, people still had as much fun as they could. Occasionally people would host "biscuit parties" where people would bring flour that they could donate to making bread or biscuits for a large group. In the South, as food shortages became severe, people would throw "starvation parties," where the only refreshment was water. Along with these types of parties, dances and dinners were put on for soldiers who came home from war for Christmas or other holidays. This, in a way, softened the war, and renewed the soldiers' energy and raised their spirits, giving them the strength to carry on through the tough times. One favorite party activity was a taffy pull. People would make a batch of taffy, butter their hands and choose partners, and pull the taffy until it was light and lost its elasticity. Taffy pulls became major social events for unmarried men and women, although during the war most taffy pulls became women-only since so many men were serving in the military.

MAKE YOUR OWN FRUIT DEHYDRATOR

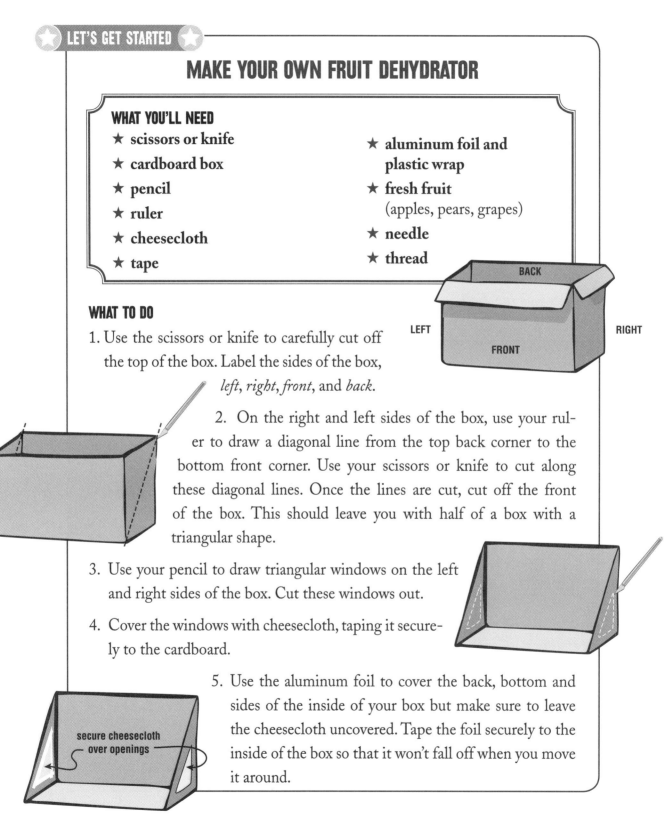

WHAT YOU'LL NEED
- ★ scissors or knife
- ★ cardboard box
- ★ pencil
- ★ ruler
- ★ cheesecloth
- ★ tape
- ★ aluminum foil and plastic wrap
- ★ fresh fruit (apples, pears, grapes)
- ★ needle
- ★ thread

BACK

LEFT

RIGHT

FRONT

WHAT TO DO

1. Use the scissors or knife to carefully cut off the top of the box. Label the sides of the box, *left*, *right*, *front*, and *back*.

2. On the right and left sides of the box, use your ruler to draw a diagonal line from the top back corner to the bottom front corner. Use your scissors or knife to cut along these diagonal lines. Once the lines are cut, cut off the front of the box. This should leave you with half of a box with a triangular shape.

3. Use your pencil to draw triangular windows on the left and right sides of the box. Cut these windows out.

4. Cover the windows with cheesecloth, taping it securely to the cardboard.

secure cheesecloth over openings

5. Use the aluminum foil to cover the back, bottom and sides of the inside of your box but make sure to leave the cheesecloth uncovered. Tape the foil securely to the inside of the box so that it won't fall off when you move it around.

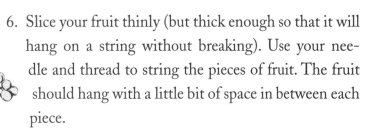

tape foil inside

6. Slice your fruit thinly (but thick enough so that it will hang on a string without breaking). Use your needle and thread to string the pieces of fruit. The fruit should hang with a little bit of space in between each piece.

7. Cut two very small holes on either side of the box above the cheesecloth screens. Thread the string through these holes so that the fruit hangs inside the dehydrator. Place tape over the holes so that nothing can get into the box.

String fruit and hang inside

8. Now that your fruit is hanging, you can cover the front of your box with plastic wrap. Secure it with tape, making the box fairly airtight (be careful to leave the cheesecloth uncovered).

secure plastic wrap over front

9. Dry your fruit! The best way to do this is to set the fruit out in the sun every day for three or four days. Bring it inside at night so that it doesn't get too cold or eaten by a wild animal.

Note: You may need to start with a larger quantity of fruit than you think; it shrinks down when it dries! Also, soaking the fruit in a mixture of 1 cup of lemon juice and 1 quart of water will help prevent browning of the fruit. However, people probably didn't have access to lemon juice during the Civil War, and most likely didn't really care if their fruit was brown.

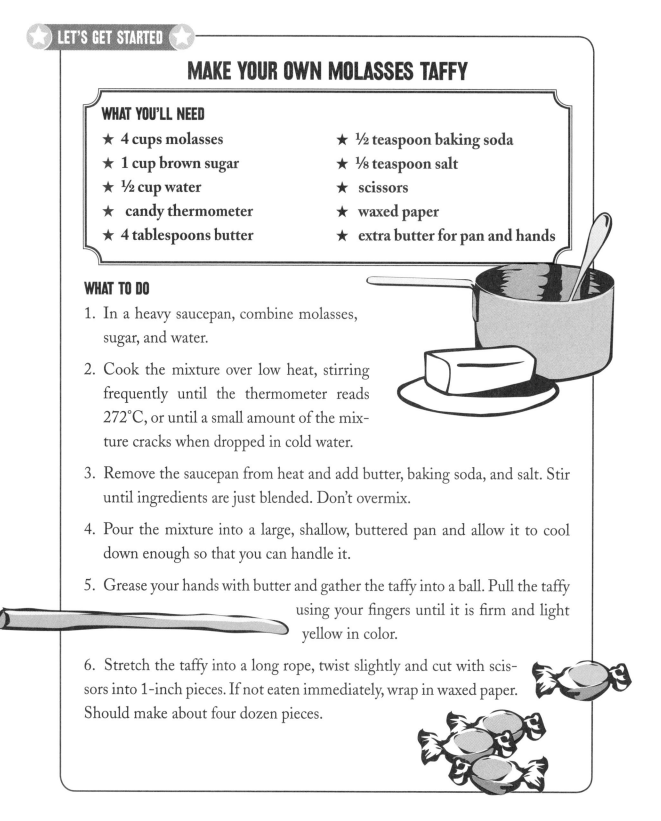

MAKE YOUR OWN MOLASSES TAFFY

WHAT YOU'LL NEED

★ 4 cups molasses

★ 1 cup brown sugar

★ ½ cup water

★ candy thermometer

★ 4 tablespoons butter

★ ½ teaspoon baking soda

★ ⅛ teaspoon salt

★ scissors

★ waxed paper

★ extra butter for pan and hands

WHAT TO DO

1. In a heavy saucepan, combine molasses, sugar, and water.

2. Cook the mixture over low heat, stirring frequently until the thermometer reads 272°C, or until a small amount of the mixture cracks when dropped in cold water.

3. Remove the saucepan from heat and add butter, baking soda, and salt. Stir until ingredients are just blended. Don't overmix.

4. Pour the mixture into a large, shallow, buttered pan and allow it to cool down enough so that you can handle it.

5. Grease your hands with butter and gather the taffy into a ball. Pull the taffy using your fingers until it is firm and light yellow in color.

6. Stretch the taffy into a long rope, twist slightly and cut with scissors into 1-inch pieces. If not eaten immediately, wrap in waxed paper. Should make about four dozen pieces.

MAKE YOUR OWN ROCK CANDY

Rock candy is another sweet that has been around since the Civil War. Depending on where they lived, people made rock candy from cane sugar, beet sugar, or maple sugar.

WHAT YOU'LL NEED

- ★ **string**
- ★ **pencil**
- ★ **clear glass or plastic jar**
- ★ **1 cup water**
- ★ **2 cups granulated sugar**
- ★ **candy flavoring** such as peppermint, cherry, or lemon (optional)
- ★ **food coloring**

WHAT TO DO

1. Tie one end of the piece of string around the pencil. Cut the string so it won't touch the bottom of the jar when the pencil is laid across the opening.

2. Wet the string and roll it in sugar. Lay the pencil over the top of the jar so the string hangs down inside the jar. Don't let the string stick to the jar sides.

3. Bring the sugar and water to a boil, stirring so that the sugar dissolves.

4. Remove from heat as soon as it boils; stir in the food coloring and flavor.

5. Pour the mixture into the jar.

6. Let the sugar water sit for a few days in a sunny window. The sun will help the water evaporate faster.

7. You should start seeing crystals develop in a few hours, but let it sit for at least three days. The crystals will grow larger the longer you leave the string in the jar.

CIVIL WAR FASHION

Although shortages of fabric and other dress goods during the Civil War meant that many women, especially those in the South, had to make changes in the way they dressed, fashions were still important in both the North and the South—women just had to make modifications based on their circumstances.

Fashions in the 1860s focused on accentuating a woman's waist, and most dresses featured a fitted bodice with wide, somewhat puffy sleeves to make their shoulders look broader and even wider hips (think hoop skirts) to showcase a tiny waist. As the war dragged on and fabric became harder and harder to find, hoop skirts went out of fashion since so much fabric was required to cover the hoops.

Women always wore their hair long, but pinned up, and they rarely left the house without a bonnet on. Bonnets were primarily used to frame a woman's face, rather than protect her from the sun. Bonnet

Fashion of the 1860s.

THE LANGUAGE OF THE FAN

The idea that fans can convey messages in a kind of "fan language" has been around since the eighteenth century, and there are many written records for deciphering coded messages sent by fan. For instance, it is said that if you place your fan near your heart, it means that you love the person this gesture is directed toward. If you fan quickly, you're engaged to be married, while if you fan slowly, you are already married. Holding your fan half opened at your lips means that you would like to be kissed, and if you open and close your fan several times it means that you think the person you directed your motion toward was cruel.

fashions changed over the war years, too, with bonnets getting smaller and smaller as the years went by, eventually being replaced by small hats.

Most women, especially in the South, carried fans with them to cool off during the hot and humid months (with no air conditioning). Fans also had an underlying purpose: wordless communication. With different movements of the fan, a woman could give unspoken messages to the person she was talking to, to a person across the room, or to a man from whom she desired attention. This allowed her to communicate without appearing too forward, an undesireable trait for women in the Civil War era.

One of the most popular forms of fashion during the 1860s was "mourning fashion." Mourning fashion was popularized by England's Queen Victoria, whose husband, Prince Albert, died in 1861, just as the American Civil War was beginning. Queen Victoria dressed in black mourning

Typical dress of 1860s.

Cameo.

clothes to memorialize her husband and required her staff to wear all black, as well. In fact, she wore mourning clothes for more than forty years, and sparked a fashion trend that jumped across the Atlantic Ocean and coincided with a time when many American women would experience the death of a loved one.

Mourning "dress" wasn't just a black dress: it extended to bonnets, hats, veils, handkerchiefs, shoes, and any other piece of clothing seen in public. Businesses specialized in selling only black clothing. Mourning apparel extended to jewelry, as well, with mourning jewelry usually made of black jet or gutta-percha (a substance made from tree sap that looked black when it hardened). Lockets and cameos, while not mourning jewelry, were also very much in fashion, and women would often carry around locks of hair given to them by their husbands, sons, or sweethearts.

Southern women in typical dress gathered to sew uniforms.

CIVIL WAR FACTS & TRIVIA

★ *Clothes worn by women were quite impractical, with the long trailing skirts nearly impossible to keep clean.*

★ *Young women who wore hoop skirts were known as "tilters" because of the skirt's tendency to rise up or tilt in the back.*

★ *Many women campaigned for dress reform, arguing that the corset, which cinched in the waist as tightly as possible, was bad for a woman's health.*

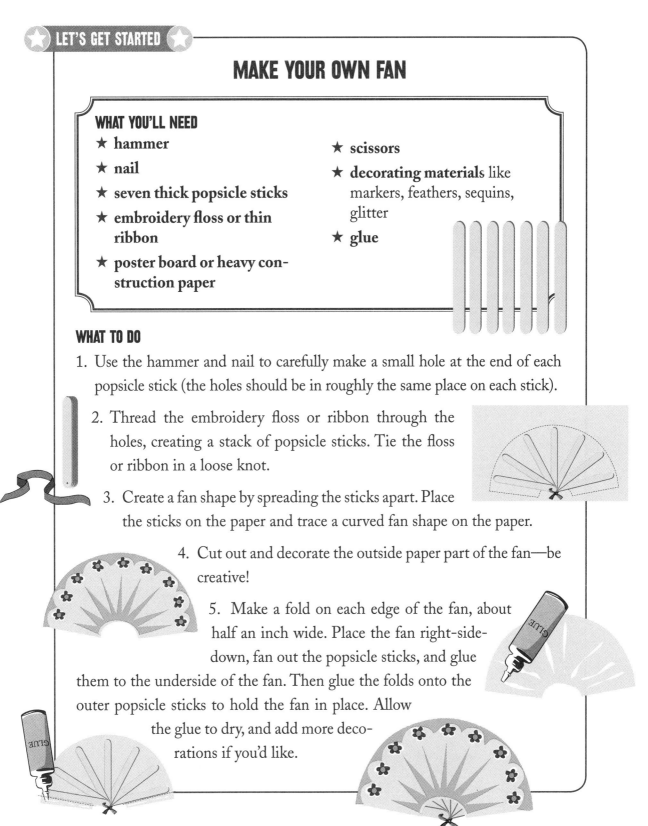

★ LET'S GET STARTED ★

MAKE YOUR OWN FAN

WHAT YOU'LL NEED
- ★ hammer
- ★ nail
- ★ seven thick popsicle sticks
- ★ embroidery floss or thin ribbon
- ★ poster board or heavy construction paper
- ★ scissors
- ★ decorating materials like markers, feathers, sequins, glitter
- ★ glue

WHAT TO DO

1. Use the hammer and nail to carefully make a small hole at the end of each popsicle stick (the holes should be in roughly the same place on each stick).

2. Thread the embroidery floss or ribbon through the holes, creating a stack of popsicle sticks. Tie the floss or ribbon in a loose knot.

3. Create a fan shape by spreading the sticks apart. Place the sticks on the paper and trace a curved fan shape on the paper.

4. Cut out and decorate the outside paper part of the fan—be creative!

5. Make a fold on each edge of the fan, about half an inch wide. Place the fan right-side-down, fan out the popsicle sticks, and glue them to the underside of the fan. Then glue the folds onto the outer popsicle sticks to hold the fan in place. Allow the glue to dry, and add more decorations if you'd like.

MAKE YOUR OWN CAMEO

Cameos are pieces of jewelry that have a raised image on a flat background. The image usually is the head of a woman, but your cameo subject can be anything, from your favorite cat to your bike.

WHAT YOU'LL NEED

★ **black modeling clay**

★ **white or ivory modeling clay**

★ **rolling pin**

★ **pin back** (or a safety pin)

★ **exacto knife**

★ **glue** (model cement works best, but white glue is okay, too)

WHAT TO DO

1. Knead the black clay thoroughly and roll it thin (about ⅛-inch thick)

2. Trace an oval about 3 inches tall by 2 inches wide (see diagram) onto the clay, and cut out the oval using the exacto knife. This will be the base for your cameo.

about ⅛″

3. Use the white or ivory clay to create an image for your cameo. It will lie flat on the black background, so make sure it fits in the black oval. Score the black clay where the white clay will meet it so they will adhere to each other better.

4. Press the cameo onto the black background and bake per the instructions on the clay packet.

5. When the clay is cool and dry, turn it over and glue the pin backing or safety pin to the back.

POPULAR MUSIC

The most popular music in America during the Civil War was called minstrel music, which was based on two musical traditions: African and Celtic (Irish and Scottish). Minstrel music featured four main instruments: banjos, fiddles, tambourines, and the bones (literally, two pig or cow rib bones). Banjos were first brought to America by African slaves in the late seventeenth century, and their music became part of the culture of the South. Most of the white South was settled by Scottish and Irish immigrants, and they brought their musical traditions of Celtic fiddle songs with them, as well. The mixture of the two brought about the musical traditions that have become uniquely American, including the blues, bluegrass, country, ragtime, and Dixieland.

Minstrel music was also based on an ugly tradition called "blackface," which had been part of American music since Colonial times. Minstrels were white people who blacked their faces, exaggerated their speech, and performed on stage while pretending to be (and ridiculing) black people. It's surprising to us now that something so mean spirited and racist could have lasted so long, but minstrel music was the most popu-

Banjo player in traditional "blackface" from a minstrel show.

"Bones" player.

lar form of music in America for almost thirty years before and during the Civil War.

Minstrel shows usually consisted of three parts: the first part was a traditional song recital, where members of the whole minstrel troupe sang popular songs such as "Old Folks at Home" and "Camptown Races," and told jokes and riddles. The second part of the show was more of a variety act, where individual performers would come on stage one at a time and do separate acts. The third part was usually a skit that combined acting and songs that commented on current events.

Minstrel shows first became popular in the 1840s, when a group called the Virginia Minstrels toured the country, playing music and performing skits. The Virginia Minstrels were such a hit that they caused a minstrel craze that peaked right around the time of the Civil War. Hundreds of minstrel troupes performed in cities all over the country, and minstrel music was played by anyone who could pick up a banjo, fiddle, or bones.

CIVIL WAR FACTS & TRIVIA

★ *Plantation owners would sometimes send slaves with musical talent to New Orleans or up North to be trained on violin so they could play at parties and dances.*

★ *Black folk music was also called "contraband" music, and was music sung or played by slaves on Southern plantations. Many Northerners heard this type of music for the first time during the Civil War, and incorporated its style and sound (like being sung in a minor key) into new musical styles, such as the blues, after the war.*

★ *The most famous white banjo player during the Civil War was a man named Sam Sweeney, who was an orderly for Confederate General J.E.B. Stuart.*

★ *Banjos have had several other names, including banjar, bangie, and banza.*

Depiction of a boy
with a banjo.

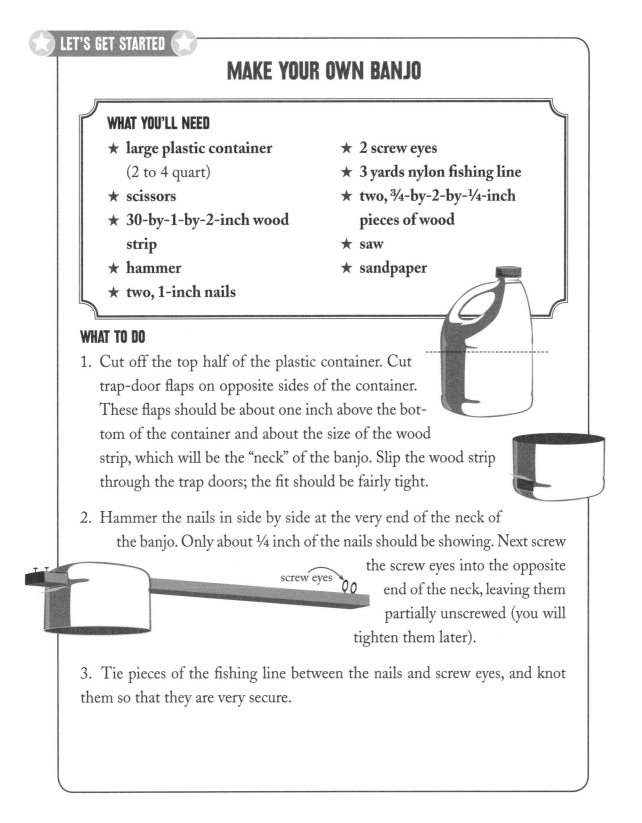

MAKE YOUR OWN BANJO

WHAT YOU'LL NEED

- ★ large plastic container (2 to 4 quart)
- ★ scissors
- ★ 30-by-1-by-2-inch wood strip
- ★ hammer
- ★ two, 1-inch nails
- ★ 2 screw eyes
- ★ 3 yards nylon fishing line
- ★ two, ¾-by-2-by-¼-inch pieces of wood
- ★ saw
- ★ sandpaper

WHAT TO DO

1. Cut off the top half of the plastic container. Cut trap-door flaps on opposite sides of the container. These flaps should be about one inch above the bottom of the container and about the size of the wood strip, which will be the "neck" of the banjo. Slip the wood strip through the trap doors; the fit should be fairly tight.

2. Hammer the nails in side by side at the very end of the neck of the banjo. Only about ¼ inch of the nails should be showing. Next screw the screw eyes into the opposite end of the neck, leaving them partially unscrewed (you will tighten them later).

screw eyes

3. Tie pieces of the fishing line between the nails and screw eyes, and knot them so that they are very secure.

4. Take one of the smaller pieces of wood (this piece will make the "bridge") and insert it under the strings at the point where the strings cross the center of the bottom of the plastic container. Cut string-size grooves in the bridge so that the strings can sit securely on the bridge.

5. Place the other small piece of wood under the strings next to the screw eyes. This will give the strings extra tension. In order to tighten the strings, screw the screw eyes in tighter. Strings should be tight for maximum resonance.

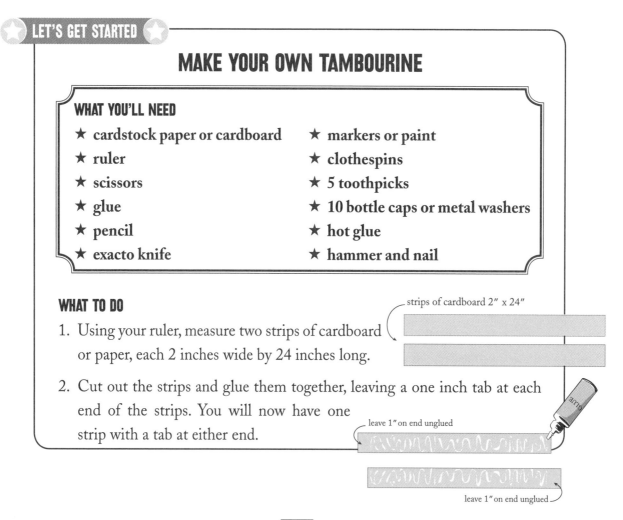

nails

piece of wood for bridge

screw eyes

fishing line

LET'S GET STARTED

MAKE YOUR OWN TAMBOURINE

WHAT YOU'LL NEED
- ★ cardstock paper or cardboard
- ★ ruler
- ★ scissors
- ★ glue
- ★ pencil
- ★ exacto knife
- ★ markers or paint
- ★ clothespins
- ★ 5 toothpicks
- ★ 10 bottle caps or metal washers
- ★ hot glue
- ★ hammer and nail

WHAT TO DO

1. Using your ruler, measure two strips of cardboard or paper, each 2 inches wide by 24 inches long.

strips of cardboard 2″ x 24″

2. Cut out the strips and glue them together, leaving a one inch tab at each end of the strips. You will now have one strip with a tab at either end.

leave 1″ on end unglued

GLUE

leave 1″ on end unglued

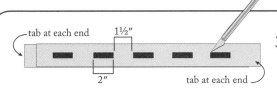

tab at each end · 1½″ · 2″ · tab at each end

3. Using your pencil, draw five rectangles on the strip, each about 1½ inches apart. Each rectangle should be about half an inch wide by 2 inches long. Using your scissors or exacto knife, cut out the rectangles. Paint or color to decorate your tambourine.

4. Next, bend the strip into a circle and glue the tabs together. Use your clothespins to hold the tabs together until the glue dries. If the tambourine needs to be stronger, you can add another piece of paper or cardboard at the seam.

5. Cut off the sharp ends of your five toothpicks, and put each toothpick through two washers. If you are using bottle caps, use a hammer and nail to punch a hole through the caps and place two on each toothpick. Using the hot glue, glue the toothpicks in the center of each rectangle cut-out and allow to dry.

hot glue toothpicks

CIVIL WAR FACTS & TRIVIA

★ *Banjos brought to America by slaves were made of gourds, wood, and tanned skins, with hemp or gut for the strings. During the Civil War, soldiers would use whatever supplies they could find to make simple banjos to play in camp. They would sometimes sneak into drummers' tents and make a hole in the head of a drum, then wait until the drummers threw out the drum head. Then they would use it for their banjos.*

THE UNDERGROUND RAILROAD

The Underground Railroad was started well before the Civil War began, but was in full force during the first years of the war. Established around 1830, this "railroad" didn't consist of trains, of course, but of a network of houses and other safe havens for slaves escaping from the South to the North. These safe places were called "stations" and guides were called "conductors." Slaves learned about routes to freedom by word of mouth and through stories and songs, including "Follow the Drinking Gourd," which explained how to follow the North Star of the Big Dipper north to Canada.

The Fugitive Slave Act of 1850 made escaping slavery dangerous not only for slaves, but also for abolitionists and free blacks in the North. The Fugitive Slave Act made it illegal for anyone to help runaway slaves, and stiff fines and punishments were given to people found to be harboring or helping slaves running to freedom. Slave catchers from the South who traveled to northern cities to capture escaped slaves also kidnapped free black people and brought them back south, as well. The catchers could make

Fugitive slaves fording the Rappahannock River, Rappahannock, Virginia, August 1862.

great money collecting rewards for fugitive slaves—and since most free blacks had little or no documentation of their status, they were easily stolen and resold as slaves back in the South. This was a disaster for free black communities in the North, but it also helped create a sense of outrage in Northerners, many of whom had previously turned a blind eye to the issue of slavery. The worst punishments,

Harriet Tubman (far left) with slaves she helped during the Civil War.

obviously, came to slaves who were caught and returned to their slave owners, and, in fact, only a fraction of the millions of slaves who lived in the South before the Civil War ever tried to escape. The slaves who stayed fought slavery in their own, more subtle ways: working as slowly as possible, having various "sicknesses," and sabotaging farm equipment and machinery.

Stations on the Underground Railroad were marked by a wide variety of signals to indicate whether or not the house was safe for fugitive slaves to enter. Some of these signals have been checked out by historians and proven to be true, and others have

HARRIET TUBMAN

Perhaps the most famous person involved in the Underground Railroad was Harriet Tubman, also known to many runaway slaves as "Moses." She was born into slavery in Maryland and escaped to Philadelphia in 1849 when she was a young woman. She worked there as a maid, and soon became involved in helping to free other slaves through the Underground Railroad. She was one of the most wanted fugitives, and rewards for her capture were thousands of dollars. She traveled back to the South multiple times, and in her first trip she managed to bring her sister and her sister's children back to Philadelphia with her. By the time the Civil War was over, Harriet Tubman had helped more than 50 slaves escape to freedom.

Harriet Tubman

THE AMERICAN COLONIZATION SOCIETY

In 1816, two divided groups of Americans met and formed the American Coloniza-tion Society: one was made up primarily of Southerners who wanted to keep African Americans as slaves but wanted freed slaves out of America; the other was primarily Northerners who wanted to free all the slaves, but wanted them to return to Africa. Both groups had one thing in common: neither believed that free African Americans could join the white culture in America or become a significant part of society. The American Colonization Society raised money to send free blacks back to Africa.

For more than 20 years, the American Colonization Society worked to resettle for-mer slaves in Africa, forming the colony of Liberia. In 1847, a black governor was elected, making Liberia the first nation in Africa to be governed by a black person. By 1860, about 11,000 blacks had been transported to Liberia, but after 1865 African American interest in emigrating waned.

LIBERIA

been part of stories for so many years that they are assumed to be true. One signal that has been verified by historians as indicating a safe stop on the Underground Railroad is a lantern hanging on a hitching post outside an established safe house. If the lan-tern was lit, it meant it was safe to approach. If the lantern was out, it was too danger-ous to knock on the door. Other signals that may or may not really have been used to indicate a house safe to enter include smoke coming out of the chimney, a chimney with white bricks placed on top of it, or a lawn statue by the side of the drive holding a flag in its hand—if the flag was missing, it was not safe to enter.

CIVIL WAR FACTS & TRIVIA

★ *Slaves used a hollowed out gourd to scoop water out of a bucket to drink. They called the Big Dipper the Drinking Gourd.*

★ *The song "Follow the Drinking Gourd" gave cooded directions for slaves escaping from Alabama and Mississippi, telling them to leave in the winter, where and when to cross the rivers, and where to meet guides to lead them to Canada.*

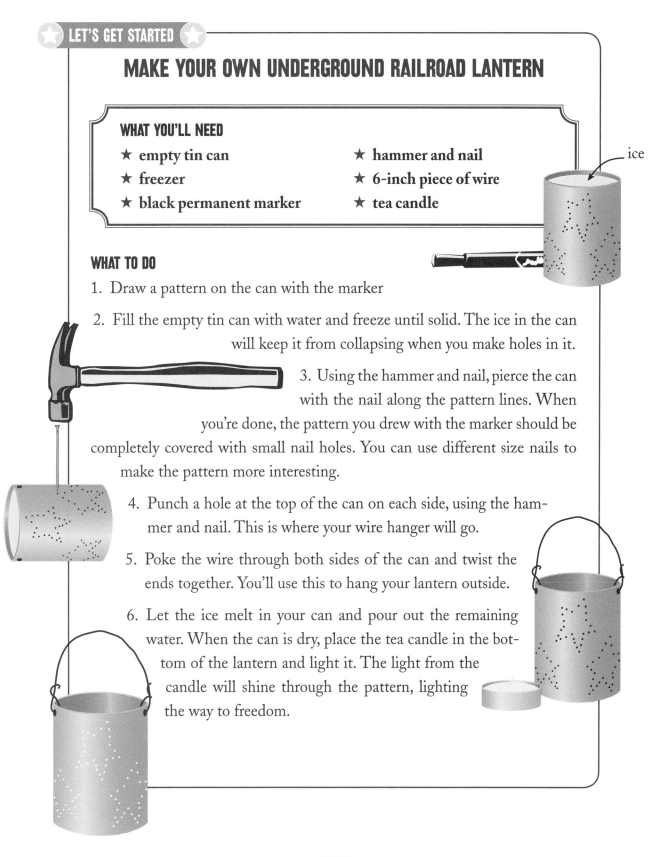

MAKE YOUR OWN UNDERGROUND RAILROAD LANTERN

WHAT YOU'LL NEED
- ★ empty tin can
- ★ freezer
- ★ black permanent marker
- ★ hammer and nail
- ★ 6-inch piece of wire
- ★ tea candle

ice

WHAT TO DO

1. Draw a pattern on the can with the marker

2. Fill the empty tin can with water and freeze until solid. The ice in the can will keep it from collapsing when you make holes in it.

3. Using the hammer and nail, pierce the can with the nail along the pattern lines. When you're done, the pattern you drew with the marker should be completely covered with small nail holes. You can use different size nails to make the pattern more interesting.

4. Punch a hole at the top of the can on each side, using the hammer and nail. This is where your wire hanger will go.

5. Poke the wire through both sides of the can and twist the ends together. You'll use this to hang your lantern outside.

6. Let the ice melt in your can and pour out the remaining water. When the can is dry, place the tea candle in the bottom of the lantern and light it. The light from the candle will shine through the pattern, lighting the way to freedom.

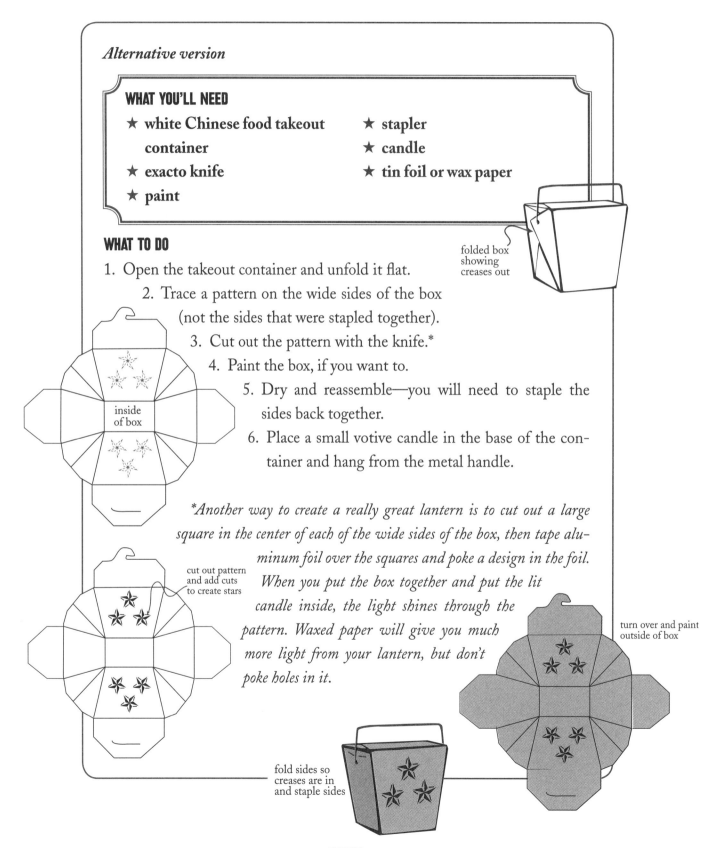

Alternative version

WHAT YOU'LL NEED

★ white Chinese food takeout container

★ exacto knife

★ paint

★ stapler

★ candle

★ tin foil or wax paper

folded box showing creases out

WHAT TO DO

1. Open the takeout container and unfold it flat.

2. Trace a pattern on the wide sides of the box (not the sides that were stapled together).

3. Cut out the pattern with the knife.*

4. Paint the box, if you want to.

5. Dry and reassemble—you will need to staple the sides back together.

6. Place a small votive candle in the base of the container and hang from the metal handle.

inside of box

Another way to create a really great lantern is to cut out a large square in the center of each of the wide sides of the box, then tape aluminum foil over the squares and poke a design in the foil. When you put the box together and put the lit candle inside, the light shines through the pattern. Waxed paper will give you much more light from your lantern, but don't poke holes in it.

cut out pattern and add cuts to create stars

turn over and paint outside of box

fold sides so creases are in and staple sides

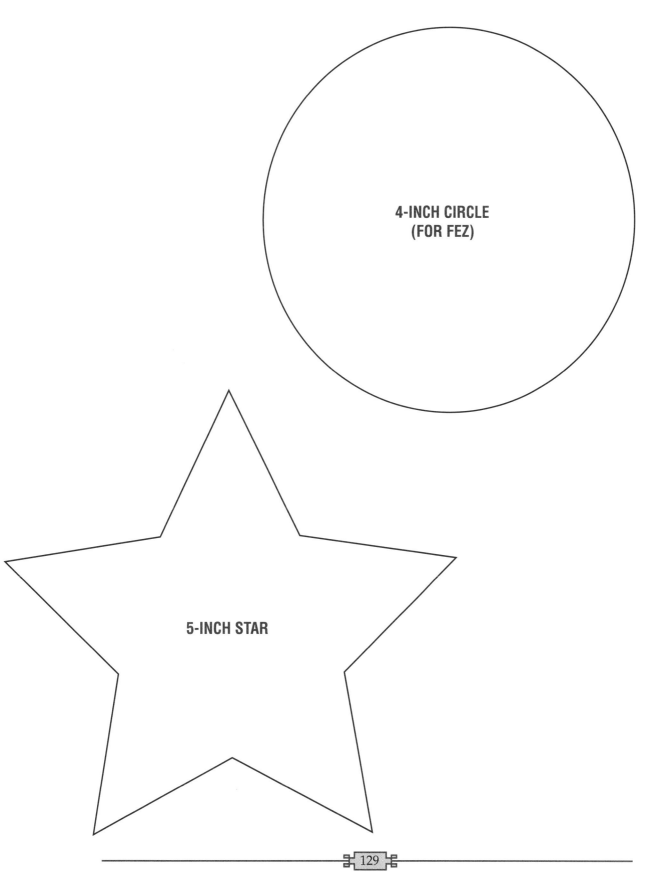

4-INCH CIRCLE
(FOR FEZ)

5-INCH STAR

**ALLOW FOR MORE SPACE HERE WHEN
TRANSFERRING THIS ONTO PILLOWCASE**

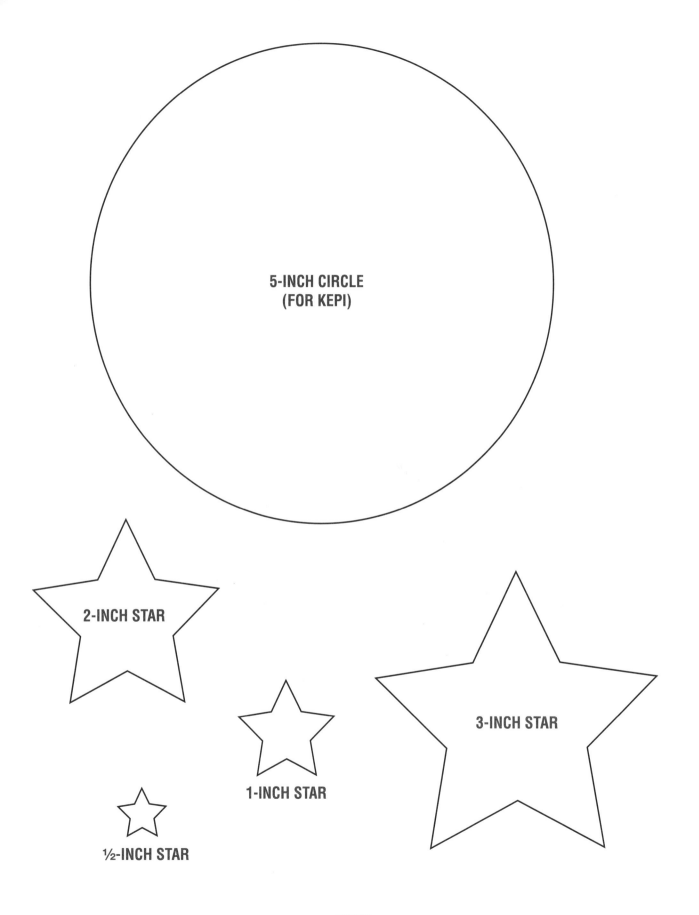

5-INCH CIRCLE
(FOR KEPI)

2-INCH STAR

1-INCH STAR

½-INCH STAR

3-INCH STAR

4⅞-INCH SQUARE
(FOR QUILT)

2½-INCH SQUARE
(FOR QUILT)

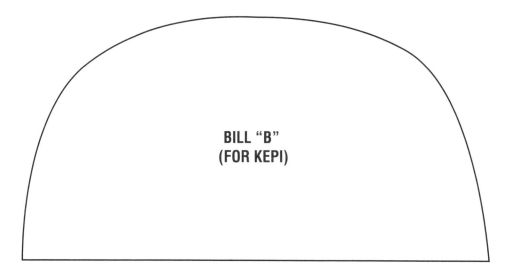

BILL "B"
(FOR KEPI)

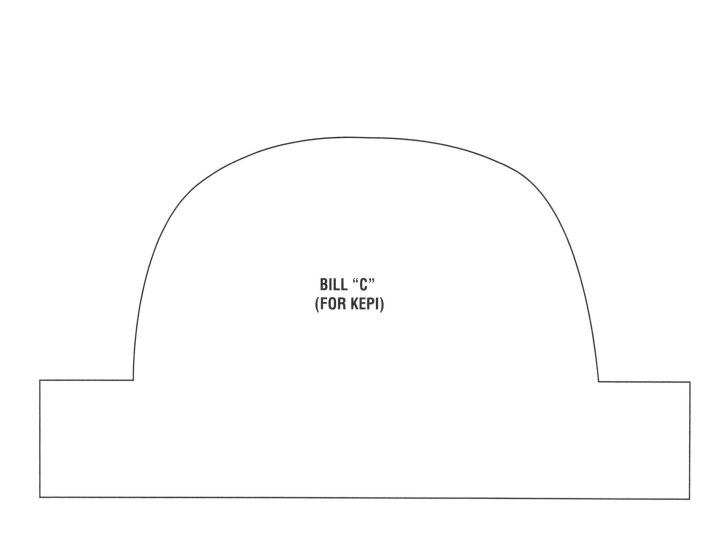

BILL "C"
(FOR KEPI)

abolitionist: someone who believed that slavery should be abolished.

artillery: division of the army that handles large weapons.

bombproof: an underground shelter; also an officer or soldier who never went to the front.

bread basket: stomach.

Bummer: a loafer, a forager, or someone safe in the rear.

Bummer's cap: regulation fatigue or forage cap.

California 100: a group of 100 men from California, originally from the East Coast, who joined a Massachusetts cavalry regiment but had their own uniform, flag, and equipment.

casualty: a soldier injured, killed, captured, or missing in action.

cavalry: soldiers trained to fight on horseback.

chicken guts: officer's gold braiding on his cuff.

Confederate: the government established by the southern states of the United States after they seceded from the Union in 1860 and 1861, called the Confederate States of America.

dragoons: heavily armed subdivisions of the cavalry.

duds: clothing.

Federal: having to do with the northern United States and those loyal to the Union during the Civil War; also a member of the Union army.

fit as a fiddle: in good shape, healthy, feeling good.

fresh fish: new recruits.

front: the area where the military is fighting.

goobers: peanuts.

grab a root: have dinner of a potato.

Graybacks: Southern soldiers.

hayfoot, strawfoot: command used to teach new soldiers the difference between left (hayfoot) and right (strawfoot).

here's your mule: a term the infantry used to insult the cavalry.

hornets: bullets.

hospital rat: person who fakes illness.

housewife: sewing kit.

infantry: soldiers trained to fight on foot.

jawings: talking.

long sweetening: molasses.

opening of the ball: units waiting to move into battle.

picket line: the line between Confederate and Union soldiers on the battlefield.

picket: a guard or guard duty.

possum: buddy.

sawbones: surgeon.

siege fighting: long battles where troops hunker down in trenches and fortifications, for several days to several months, fighting only sporadically.

snug as a bug: very comfortable or cozy.

somebody's darling: a dead soldier; also the name of a popular Civil War song.

sutler: army camp follower who peddles provisions to the soldiers.

top rail: first class, the best.

Union: the United States of America, especially the northern states during the American Civil War.

vittles: food or rations.

web feet: a term the cavalry had for the infantry.

wig-wag: a letter–number code represented by certain positions and movements of a

signal flag: Used to communicate on the battlefield.

Zouave: comes from an Algerian word for soldiers known for their fierce fighting style, flashy uniforms, and incredible bravery. Units devoted to the Zouave style fought in both the Union and Confederate armies during the Civil War.

Zuzu: Zouaves.

RESOURCES

BOOKS

Beard, D.C. *The American Boy's Handy Book*. David Godine, 1998.

Bolotin, Norman. *Civil War A to Z: A Young Readers' Guide to Over 100 People, Places, and Points of Importance.* Dutton Children's Books, New York, 2002.

Brackman, Barbara. *Quilts from the Civil War.* C&T Publishing, Lafayette, California, 1997.

Chang, Ina. *A Separate Battle: Women and the Civil War.* From *Young Readers' History of the Civil War series.* Lodestar Books, New York, 1991.

Corrick, James A. *Life among the Soldiers and Cavalry. The Civil War series,* Lucent Books, San Diego, 2000.

Currie, Stephen. *Women of the Civil War. Women in History series,* Lucent Books, 2003.

Damon, Duane. *When This Cruel War is Over: The Civil War Home Front.* Lerner Publications, Minneapolis, 1996.

Davis, Burke. *The Civil War: Strange & Fascinating Facts.* Wings Books, New York, 1996.

Hakim, Joy. *A History of US: War, Terrible War (Volume 6).* Oxford University Press, 2002.

Hesse, Karen. *A Light in the Storm: The Civil War Diary of Amelia Martin. Dear America series.* Scholastic, New York, 1999.

Langellier, John P. *Terrible Swift Sword: Union Artillery, Cavalry, and Infantry, 1861-1865.* Chelsea House Publishers, Philadelphia, 2002.

Luchetti, Cathy. *Medicine Women: The Story of Early-American Women Doctors.* Crown, New York, 1998.

McPherson, James M. *Fields of Fury: the American Civil War.* Atheneum Books for Young readers, New York, 2002.

Murphy, Jim. *The Boys' War.* Clarion Books, 2002.

O'Brien, Patrick. *Duel of the Ironclads: The Monitor vs. The Virginia.* Walker & Company, New York, 2003.

Rappaport, Doreen. *No More! Stories and Songs of Slave Resistance.* Candlewick Press, Cambridge, Massachusetts, 2002.

Roca, Steven Louis. "Presence and precedents: The USS Red Rover during the American Civil War, 1861-1865." *Civil War History*, July 1998.

Varhola, Michael J. *Everyday Life During the Civil War.* Writer's Digest Books, 1999.

WEB SITES
University and Government Sites

Civil War Index Page at Dakota State University:
www.homepages.dsu.edu/jankej/civilwar/civilwar.htm

Library of Congress Civil War Photographs:
http://memory.loc.gov/ammem/cwphtml/cwphome.html

National Civil War Museum: www.nationalcivilwarmuseum.org

National Park Service site (includes sections on many Civil War park sites):
www.nps.gov

United States Civil War Center: www.cwc.lsu.edu/

Privately Held Sites

www.americancivilwar.com

www.civil-war.net

www.teacheroz.com/civilwar.htm